AWAKENING THROUGH GRIEF

A Spiritual Journey of Healing and Transformation After Loss

ANGELA CLEMENT

ISBN Paperback: # 978-1-0690759-0-1
ISBN Electronic: # 978-1-0690759-1-8

Publishing Consultant: PRESStinely, PRESStinely.com

Portions of this book are works of nonfiction. Certain names and identifying characteristics have been changed.

Printed in the United States of America.

Awaken Your Soul's Journey
www.healingenergy.world

To my husband, Blaine.
Your love, trust, and devotion have made me who I am today.
Only you and I know this unique bond.
You continue to be the meaning and the inspiration
as I embrace this life with you tucked deep inside my heart.
This love is forever,
Angela

*Grief can be the garden of compassion.
If you keep your heart open through everything,
your pain can become your greatest ally
in your life's search for love and wisdom.*[1]
—Rumi

Foreword

by Julie Cluff

Grief is an astonishing emotion. It catches us off guard, knocks us off balance, and forcefully invites us to reexamine every assumption we have made about life up to that point. Despite the truth that loss and grief have been present since the dawn of humanity, society is still woefully ignorant about grief and how to approach this very personal, complex emotion.

As a community, largely, we still see grief as damaging. We view grief predominantly as an unwelcome guest we must entertain and invite into every space of our existence for the rest of our lives. This unbalanced, destructive, and pervasive perception of grief is the reason the book you hold in your hand is so important. This book invites you to reconsider these repeatedly held interpretations of grief. This is a millennial exposé of grief healing, written by a hands-on seeker, who understands personally that grief is a part of the healing process.

I met Angela in the first year of her grief after the death of her beloved Blaine. I was at once struck by her insatiable hunger for answers to the pain she was feeling. She fought against the idea that grief would last forever and at the same time feared it might be true. She was determined to find the answers.

While grief invites transformation, it also invites contemplation. In her own path of discovery, she found joy again and proved her hypothesis that grief does not have to last forever. Angela invites you to reexamine your assumptions about grief and introduces the hopeful models of grief as a path to healing from upheaval. There is no better guide than someone who is familiar with the path.

I have also felt the devastating effects of loss and grief. After my beautiful children, David, age eight, and Carrie, age ten, died in a rollover car accident, I was faced with the shock and horror of crushing loss and grief. Years before that tragic event, my brother died by suicide and my first marriage ended in divorce; both paradigm-shifting events. When I reflected on the resilience I experienced after my brother's death and the divorce, I wondered if it was possible that I could also heal the grief from the death of my children. This reflection gave me light in the darkness of despair. That was the beginning of my hope. That hope, along with time, understanding, effort, healing tools, and God's grace, led me to a very personal healing.

At the time of loss, the circumstances are so overwhelming that we can easily feel like the dark, heavy feelings will never leave. Numerous established, yet untrue, assumptions strengthen the societal belief that we must grieve forever after a loss. The top two "proofs" that are given for this assumption are, first, the stark reality of never being able to regain the previous circumstances of life. In other words, that which is lost cannot be recovered. This leads to the mistaken belief that because the loss cannot be recovered, the grief must remain as well. The second top societal "proof" is that love is connected to grief, and if you let go of the pain of grief, then you are letting go of the love.

The tricky entanglement of these ideas that pervade our collective belief system prolongs our suffering. Because while there is an element of truth in each statement, on further examination, the assumptions fall apart. For example, we do not need to feel grief to feel love when someone is present. If this is true—and it is—it would only make sense that, after processing the change in our circumstances through the experience of grief, we can once again feel love without the heaviness of grief.

Grief is a deeply emotional, physical, mental, and spiritual experience, and, as such, deserves our attention on all four levels. The emotional is obvious, as are the physical reactions we feel and the mental gymnastics we engage in after a loss. The spiritual or energetic impact is less obvious and less easy to define, but no less impactful. Angela's examination of grief and healing and her suggested exercises help on all four levels, which is another reason this book is so pivotal. As you read and learn, you will find answers to your questions about how to navigate the present while healing the past and approaching the future.

This is what I know. Despite that we miss the physical presence of our loved ones who have died, they continue to be present in spirit. They are lifted from the density of this earthly plane and surrounded by love and light. They are well taken care of and they are near us. Because we do not understand the realm of the spirit, it is challenging for us to comprehend how they can be there and here, but my experiences confirm my belief. From their new vantage point, our loved ones are still loving us the same as we are still loving them. They are assisting us, with the help of our other spirit guides, in our search for understanding and meaning in this new phase of life. As I've worked with hundreds of people, I've felt the influence of their loved ones who have died. I've felt their loved ones' direct involvement in the healing of their broken hearts.

The person you have lost has led you here to Angela's beautiful offering. Angela found answers to her suffering and, in her loving and compassionate way, offers you a pathway from loss to grief to hope to healing. She is a gentle voice in the landscape of hardship. She is a light in the storms of life. She is a guide down a path that is treacherous and scary when you do not understand what is happening or where you are going. What you are about to read is a map of the trail. In these pages, Angela will show you the pitfalls to avoid and the soft places to land and rest along the way.

All the best to you, my friend, as you embark on a journey we call grief and healing.

Julie Cluff, Author of *Miracles in the Darkness*, Founder of Build a Life After Loss, and Healing Coach at juliecluff.com

Acknowledgments

I would like to honor these important people in my life who have stood by me, supported me, loved me, and allowed me to become who I am. My mom and dad, Elaine and Allan; my children, Curtise and Whitney, and their spouses, Jennifer and Sheldon; my brother Calvin and his partner, Tammi; my Aunt Sharon and Uncle Don; and so many cousins who have stepped in to support me when I needed it most.

Tons of gratitude to Blaine's family for being there for me and my family and for continuing to support us through this difficult time for us all.

To my friends who continue to support me always, and especially those who have been with me through the worst. You know who you are.

To Julie Cluff, my grief coach; special healers, Roxene Harris-Swayne, Joan Tremblay, Cathleena Hailey, Ana Coeur, Adrien Blackwell, Kevin Hughes, and so many more people that have touched my life just at the right time in the most profound way. You have been divinely sent, and your compassion and caring have made a huge impact on my life.

To my mom, Elaine Winquist, for providing the EFT scripts in this book. I know so many will find them helpful.

To the Awaken Your Soul's Journey community, thank you for walking with me in my quest to bring hope, comfort, and healing to those in grief.

To my amazing editor, Michael Ireland. How wonderful to find you! You brought out my best. I am so grateful for your expertise and your encouragement.

To every doctor, nurse, coach, healer, and mentor that makes it their priority to help those who grieve. You are earth angels. Please know you are making a difference every single day.

—Angela

Table of Contents

Note to Reader

This book is meant to be read once through and then opened at random to specific chapters for daily inspiration and guidance; therefore, key ideas are repeated. I recommend you have a journal nearby as you read this book. Write down any insights that come from the text as well as any thoughts or emotions that come forward as you relate to your own circumstance. There are exercises at the end of each chapter to help you integrate the content and express any discomfort you may be experiencing.

You may wish to engage the services of a professional grief therapist to assist you as you are doing the work outlined in this book. I know how difficult it can be to do this work. I also know how much easier it is with the assistance of a coach. Someone who is trained to assist those in grief can provide comfort as well as understanding when it is needed most. They can also provide affirmation that you are progressing and can recommend more resources if and when you need them. If you have financial challenges and feel you cannot afford support, please do not stop looking.

Often, we give up too soon. Allow the opportunities to find you, and when they do, say yes! Continue to search for ways to get the support you need as you continue along your journey. There are often scholarships or grants for the programs you are seeking, if you just ask the facilitators of these programs. I truly believe that everyone should have some type of support system when going through a loss. Start looking for the support and guidance you deserve right away. You are surely worthy of kind and loving support after all you have been through!

Introduction

If you have found this book, you have likely experienced loss. First, I am so sorry for your loss. Losing someone you love is extremely difficult, and you might wonder how you will ever make it through. You might ask yourself if you will ever be able to laugh or smile again. It may not seem possible. When my husband Blaine died, it felt like I was breaking in two. I had so many questions, but I did not know where to look for answers, or where to turn. I wanted Blaine back. I wanted my life back.

I was not prepared for the devastating loss of my husband, my best friend, the love of my life, and the father of our children. Blaine was my cheerleader, my confidant, my life partner. He was my rock. I had built a life with him, and we had hopes, dreams, and plans. We were inseparable, going everywhere and doing everything together. Blaine's death was the most traumatic experience of my life. I could never have imagined how gut wrenching it would be.

Only my "Blainie" will know the depth of our love or my loss. It is impossible to explain it in words. Only Blaine will ever truly understand the unique relationship we built over thirty-five years of marriage. No one will ever understand my pain—except those from above who watch over me and walked with me in my darkest hour. Still, I feel compelled to tell my story and share what I have learned with others who have experienced the loss of a profound love.

Life itself is a series of losses. Our first experience with loss happened when we were born. Releasing the old and embracing the new was part of leaving the womb. Life requires us to change, grow, and adapt. When we had to let go of the bottle, the soother, or our favorite blanket, we felt the loss. Perhaps we had a teacher we loved, and he or she moved away. We might have lost a beloved pet. We experience grief when we have to untangle ourselves from what was once familiar. Grief is a natural process that helps us let go. It got us through all the times we experienced change. Grief is integral to our lives, yet education about it is scarce. As a society, we tend not to talk about grief. We avoid it—until we have to face it directly. The loss of Blaine forced me to take notice of this process we call grief. Disturbed about what was happening to me, I wanted to understand more.

Losing Blaine catapulted me into a new trajectory in life. It all happened in its own divine timing. Resistance just caused pain and suffering. I believe there is a higher power— you might refer to it as God, the Universe, Source, Creator, or something else. From this point forward, I will refer to this connection as "God," "the Universe," or "the higher self." When I did not know what else to do, I let go of the need to control and allowed the process of grief and my higher self to guide me. The more I let go, the more my life changed in beautiful ways I never could have imagined.

After losing Blaine, I felt like no one understood. I felt alone. Though it feels that way, I want you to know that you are never alone. When we cannot hold ourselves together, eventually grief helps us see ourselves as part of a larger community. Grief opens us up to our dependence on others and helps us understand that our shared experience connects us. Many people walk with us on this journey.

Our grief journeys are all different. They crack our hearts wide open. We all come to understand the excruciating pain of loss in our own way. Grief opens us up to feeling compassion for one another. During our grief, we discover the universe guides, protects, and loves us infinitely.

When I was writing this book, I found my way through the vast, dark depths of sadness and despair. This book is about awakening to my soul's journey. I hope it will help you see that living a life you love is possible, even if you do not believe it right now. Through my loss, I experienced a profound awakening and gained a clearer understanding of the process of grief. My prayer is that telling my story will bring you hope that one day, you, too, will find happiness again.

I have divided this book into four parts. Part I looks at our understanding of grief and the initial part of the grieving process. I talk about what I learned about grief and share my response to the loss in the first few months. After surviving the initial loss, I looked for hope. This is where my journey began. Having a sense of hope taught me that even though I was feeling awful, I knew I would feel better one day. I found others who healed and built a life they love. Hope was the key to moving forward. For me, HOPE stands for a Heart Opening to Purpose and Expansion. That is how I explain the process I went through to build my new life after loss.

In Part II, I discuss what helped me heal and open my heart. I talk about how I walked through intense grief and let go of the debilitating pain with compassion and love. I discuss the importance of feeling into and releasing our emotions and how energy healing was a big part of my healing journey.

Part III is about facing the loss and acknowledging that our lives have changed. I talk about the process of letting go of what our lives were before our loss and, at the same time, how we can take the memories and love with us on our journey. Part of this journey is accepting that our future has changed. I talk about the brain and how it adapts to change. I also provide insight and information to help the reader navigate the challenge of adjusting to a new life without their loved one.

Part IV focuses on stepping into the unknown to build a life we love. Through this process, we discover the deepest, most authentic aspect of our beings—our true selves. We discover we are both human beings and spiritual beings. Our understanding of life becomes broader and expands into more than I ever could have imagined.

As you move through this book, you will read about how I worked through the process of grief by mourning. This helped me take steps on the path to healing. Once we understand how our grief is trying to help us (not hurt us), we can embrace it rather than dread it. You may have heard the saying, "What you resist persists." It is true. Allowing and moving the energy of emotion is key to letting it go.

I used alternative energy healing, along with Western medicine, to assist me in my healing and wellness. Energy healing is a generic term for modalities that, in varying ways, tap into the energy field of our bodies. Energy flows around and through our bodies, and a disturbance in this flow can cause illness and discomfort. The healing works directly with the emotional, physical, and spiritual aspects of our beings. Depending on the modality, practitioners can pinpoint blockages and clear them, and thereby restore the body's natural healing abilities.

From an energy-healing perspective, the body strives to maintain equilibrium and promote the harmonious flow of energy throughout its various systems. For example, having a massage is a form of energy healing. Because the body is more relaxed after a massage, the energy in the body can move easily. Other types of energy healing include acupuncture, Reiki, Qi Gong, Tai Chi, and meditation. As I share my story, I speak about different energy healing systems and energy healers who provided me with tremendous support. While I understand there are different beliefs and attitudes regarding alternative healing modalities, I invite you to discover what, if anything, would be helpful to you. A massage? An acupuncture treatment? Learning to meditate? Caring for your body in a way that works for you is empowering.

My hope is that you will relate to my story and apply some of these healing techniques. I pray this book inspires you to take that initial step toward opening your heart. I believe your presence in this life has a beautiful purpose. May you allow grief to guide you to find purpose and meaning and help you expand into the life you desire to create. Lots of love, Angela

PART I

Enduring
the Initial Loss

Chapter 1

———

Understanding Grief and the Grieving Process

Will You Really Grieve for a Lifetime?

In books and on social media, it is common to hear the message that when we lose someone we love, we will have to endure that grief for a lifetime. When I was in the most pain I have ever endured, I woke up every morning with a sinking feeling. I could barely put one foot in front of the other. The message I was hearing was, "Angela, you will grieve for the rest of your life." I could not imagine it. I could not bear it.

When Blaine was diagnosed with stage 4 colon cancer, he told me he felt like someone had punched him in the gut. That feeling never went away. What he had planned for the year ahead—possibly for his whole life—was no longer possible. Chemo treatments robbed him of the opportunity to travel, the joy of everyday activities, and his well-being. Going back was not an option. For both of us, the unknown future felt like a nightmare. We had to let go of the past and our hopes for the immediate future. Anytime we must let go, we experience grief.

As I watched Blaine struggle with the disease, I felt that intense punched-in-the-gut feeling too. It was present morning and night. It clouded my thinking and dampened my joy. After he died, I longed for the past and feared the future. To me, the idea of grieving for a lifetime meant enduring daily devastation. Lessening the pain was not enough. Some say that you grow around your grief. They say you will get used to the pain and learn to accept it. You will find ways to live a fulfilling and meaningful life while carrying the grief with you. Growing around the grief was not a comfort for me. I wanted the pain of grief gone! Finding relief seemed impossible. *Will I really be stuck with this feeling for the rest of my days? How can I live without Blaine? How can anyone ease this pain?*

If you have lost a special loved one, you know this feeling. You understand. We are in a club we did not sign up for, wondering, *Why am I here?* But that "punch in the gut" does not have to define your life. It is not something you have to adjust to, and you do not have to live with it. It is not constant, and it is no longer my reality. Do I feel sad sometimes? Yes. But these brief bouts of sadness do not last. I feel a range of emotions. I live an exciting, purposeful, and joyful life.

You might wonder, *Why on earth would anyone claim that grieving lasts a lifetime?* To understand that, we need to understand the process of grief and the difficulty in defining grief.

Defining Grief: What Is Grief, Anyway?

As part of a six-month energy healing course, I was encouraged to create an online summit. I chose the topic of grief. It seemed natural, as that was what I was going through at the time. It had been six months since Blaine died, and I was still learning about the grieving process. I developed an online summit for people who had lost a loved one. I titled the summit Awaken Your Soul's Journey: How to Overcome Grief Through Healing. Over 1,200 participants registered for the event. These participants became part of the community I created, which I named the Awaken Your Soul's Journey Community. I interviewed twenty-seven speakers for the first summit, which ran over two weeks. There were a variety of experts, such as counselors, coaches, therapists, death doulas, mediums, and healers, who supported my event and shared their expertise. Each participant defined grief in their own way. Exploring each definition added more clarity to my understanding of grief. When the summit was over, I invited people from my email list to join a support group. I called these regular meetings Group Get-Togethers. In one session, I held a group discussion about defining grief. I found everyone defines their grief from their own perspective. Even the dictionary definitions vary. One definition from *The Oxford Dictionary* says grief is "a feeling of deep sadness, especially when someone dies."[2] *Merriam Webster* defines it as "a deep and poignant distress caused by or as if by bereavement."[3] *Dictionary.com* describes grief as a "keen mental suffering or distress over affliction or loss; sharp sorrow; painful regret."[4]

It makes sense that grief is difficult to define because our grief is as individual as our fingerprints. After all, we can experience grief because of losing a job, home, pet, or loved one. Grief is as distinct as the relationship you had with the person you lost. As I spent more time with grief, I came to understand it as an internalized process that takes place naturally after a loss.

Some people believe grief is sadness. It is much more than that—it is a psychological process in which we may feel any emotion, including sadness, anger, guilt, or anxiety. Often, physical issues, such as loss of appetite, fatigue, and sleep disturbances, accompany these emotional issues. Grief and mourning are often intertwined processes that occur in response to loss. Although it is common for people to use the terms synonymously, they are different processes.

While grief is the internal process of loss, mourning is the outward expression of it. Mourning can involve various cultural and religious practices, such as funerals, memorial services, or rituals. Yet it extends beyond those to include talking, writing, dancing, painting, or creating in memory of our loved one. Mourning can help individuals find meaning, comfort, and healing. When we mourn, we are helping to move the energy of our grief out and transform it into something else. Mourning is the key to healing. I think we can all agree the grief process is painful and something we would rather do without. However, here is something to consider about the grieving process that might help you feel differently about your grief.

Remember I mentioned we can reframe grief as something that can help us rather than hurt us? What if we welcome grief, knowing it is showing us our path to healing? Grief is medicine, a natural process we go through to heal from loss. Accepting grief as a fierce ally can help us move forward. Grief is the bridge that will lift us from the devastation of our initial loss. It will help us learn to navigate the intense emotions that come up for release. We will learn to take care of, love, and understand ourselves better. Through this process, we can build a new, joy-filled, purposeful life. I understand it is hard to imagine a joyful life when starting the grieving process. Healing is possible, and our bodies know how to do it naturally. We must pay attention to our emotions and listen to and connect with our body through this journey.

I have framed GRIEF into an acronym: Gently Releasing Intense Emotion to move us Forward in life. Because powerful emotions accompany grief, we must be gentle and practice self-care. Sometimes, emotions come without warning. I found it is best to surrender as they arise because holding these emotions inside will cause all kinds of problems. Emotions are energy in motion. Energy wants to move through us. If we stop our emotions from flowing, we will experience pain and discomfort. Facing our emotions and feelings frees them, opening up space for us to explore things that bring joy and a life we love.

When I look back at where I was emotionally when Blaine passed and compare it to where I am now, I find that the heaviness I felt is gone. I find myself happy and content most of the time. When it comes to dealing with any emotion, I find I have confidence and resilience. The road here was difficult, but now I understand myself and my grief. My life has become a quest to continue to unfold more of who I am as a person: *What can I be for this world?* Grief was the vehicle that transported me to this new life. Grief has transformed me.

In my case, the message that "those who grieve will grieve for a lifetime" was discouraging. Others told me I would learn to carry this loss and pain. That sounded awful. The very idea was a detriment to my healing. *Is there really no way out of the devastation I feel? Should I accept it?* Thoughts are powerful things. They control not only how we feel but how we behave. Sometimes, we have to question things that do not ring true for us.

We human beings adopt beliefs over our lifetimes of experience. Our well-meaning parents, teachers, and caregivers teach us their beliefs, and they become a part of how we live our lives. Sometimes we do not realize these beliefs are governing us, and this is why awareness is important. I am on a quest to understand what grief is. *What is true for me?* I do not pretend to know everything, but I will share what I have discovered and what I believe now. You may resonate with these beliefs or you may not. Question your beliefs—it is powerful.

Grief helps us through situations in which we need to let go. In this way, it is true that grief is with us for our lifetime. From the time we were babies through to our adulthood, grief has been there to help nudge us through change. Sometimes our attachments are strong and the grief process is intense. Other times, we can let go easily—but either way, grief is there to help us.

We never forget our loved ones are gone, nor would we want to. What *can* change is how we feel. As I focused on moving my emotions and reframing my thoughts, increasingly, I found happiness and joy. I look back on my memories of Blaine with a softness and a deep gratitude for the love that continues. Love is forever. It never dies. I have moments of sadness from time to time, but I know I can choose to return to joy. Life becomes worth living. Happiness returns. Your new normal will be as wonderful as you choose it to be. This is the power of the grieving process.

Misunderstandings About Grief

There are many misunderstandings and unhelpful beliefs surrounding grief, and we must be aware of them. Common misconceptions include:

1. *There are five stages of grief.* In her book *On Death and Dying*, prominent psychologist Dr. Elizabeth Kübler-Ross explained the so-called "five stages of grief" (denial, anger, bargaining, depression, and acceptance) to help normalize the process for those facing a life-ending diagnosis. Kübler-Ross examined patients with terminal illnesses and described the stages they went through in accepting their inevitable deaths. It was (and still is) groundbreaking research. The stages Kübler-Ross described are widely applied to grief and bereavement. While many of us have been told we can expect to go through these stages of grief, it is important to know that grief does not follow a step-by-step process. The five stages of grief are not linear. We can experience these feelings at different times and sometimes all at the same time during our grief journey. Some we may not experience them at all. We should not worry about how or when we experience them. Knowing what the five stages are can be useful as an awareness tool to help us realize all these emotions are possible and normal, but remember, Kübler-Ross did not design them as a path that all those who are grieving the loss of a loved one must travel.

2. *Grief has a timeline.* Grief has no predictable timeline, and time does not automatically heal all wounds. We cannot wait passively or stay occupied until our pain disappears. We must do the healing work. I had hoped I could do steps XYZ and the pain would be gone, but I had to accept it does not work that way. I needed to be patient. Each time I showed up for myself, healing took place. That is where hope comes in: it is a beacon of light, letting us know that the pain of the grieving process will subside when we no longer need it for letting go. Grief is a "wayshower" for each of us as we walk our

path. There need not be judgment about how long each person's path is because our path is uniquely ours.

Some people say the first year is the worst. Some say it is the second year. But why compare the length of time or intensity of our grief? Why measure the depth of love we had for our loved one? The quality of our relationship, the memories we shared, and the impact that person had on our life are unique. Judging the process in any way is not beneficial.

3. *We should follow cultural rules regarding grieving behavior.* I wondered, *How should I navigate going to the funeral home, the graveside service, the ceremony, everyday life?* Everyone's eyes would be on me. Partly it was just my perception, but I am sure people were concerned and did monitor me during this difficult time. People might tell you that you are doing well because you are accomplishing daily tasks. Some people might judge you because you cry in public (or do not cry in public). Some people might tell you to move on ... or even tell you how to move on. People might make comments about your loss that make you unsure about how to navigate your grief. What should you do? *Listen to your heart.* Do what is right for you, regardless of what others say is right or wrong.

4. *We should avoid talking about loss.* Let's debunk this idea and change the Western world! So many of us do not talk about loss. Why? We do not know how. When we have not experienced a profound loss ourselves, it can be awkward. But it is important to talk about the deceased person and their passing, and it is important to allow bereaved people to express what they are going through. We worry about making a grieving person cry. I get it. I was the same. I would never ask, "What happened?" or "How are you coping?" But when I talked to others about

what happened when Blaine died, it was therapeutic. Telling someone how I was feeling was freeing. It was what I needed. I loved hearing stories about Blaine and how people remembered him. Did it make me tear up? Sometimes—but in the best way possible. So do not worry about spending time with people who are grieving. Your presence and empathy are enough to support them. You do not need to say things to make them feel better. Just being there, listening in a caring and kind way, is more comfort than you can know.

5. *Everything about grief is sad and negative.* It does not have to be. We human beings are amazing. We can hold multiple perspectives and switch from one to another. There are two or more ways to see every situation, even for something as devastating as losing a loved one. I lost my beloved husband of thirty-five years, and nothing will change that. That is the stark reality—and it is a negative in my mind for sure. When I look at my life through this lens, it is very sad. *How could anything positive come from such a loss?* But even through this unimaginable experience, I have found positives. For example, I have a deep understanding of how precious life is. I appreciate my family, friends, and all people much more. I cherish moments of joy. I realize time is short and is not to be wasted. I focus on what is important to me. I look after myself better.

Being open to new experiences empowered me and helped me achieve unexpected things. I have set healthy boundaries, and I do not let what others think or say affect me so much anymore. I have freed myself from drama. I do not sweat the small stuff like I used to. I am dedicated to learning to help myself, and at the same time, to being of service to others. It is amazing how resilient the human spirit can be. I see it time and time again in the amazing people I meet, and I look at these beautiful people as role models for my life. We can rise above the challenges we face if we can open our perception to see both the dark and the light. It does not help to judge or resist what is. There is an impermanence of all things in nature. The seasons and the cycles of day and night are forever beginning and ending. By accepting that things are forever changing, we can develop a trust and a sense of peace, even in the face of difficult circumstances. Just as we could not have day without night, we could not know joy if we did not know sadness. Both are part of the human experience.

Exercises:

1. If you were to define your grief in words, what would you say? Think about adding to your definition as you move along in this book. Come back to it from time to time and see if it is still the same for you. There is no wrong answer!

2. My definition of grief changed a little as I learned more about myself. Learning more about yourself helps you understand what you are going through and your reactions to grief. It helps you build empathy and understanding for who you are as a person and the challenges you are facing. Schedule a little time in your day, maybe five to ten minutes, to reflect on your journey with grief so far. You may write your thoughts down or just sit in silence as you contemplate the following questions:
   - What is the biggest emotion coming up for me right now?
   - What would it take for me to accept that this is a normal part of the grieving process?
   - What small thing can I do for myself today to show myself some love and self-care?

Chapter 2

Getting the News

An Unexpected, Life-Changing Experience

A few days before Christmas in December 2020, Blaine said, "I'm not feeling well. I've got a pain in my side." He ate very little on Christmas Day, which was out of character. With the COVID-19 restrictions, it was not easy to get a medical appointment, so we contacted a doctor through a phone app. The doctor suggested we give the situation a few more days, that it might clear up on its own. We waited until after the new year. Things were not improving, so we went through the not-so-simple task of making a face-to-face appointment for the first week in January in Swift Current, which was a seventy-five-mile drive from our ranch in the small town of Val Marie. I was at work, so Blaine went to his appointment alone. I was the principal of Val Marie School, a little K-12 school ten miles south of our ranch. They booked Blaine for tests that same week, including an ultrasound and bloodwork.

On the day Blaine had his tests done, he was having lunch with his sisters and brother when the doctor called him to come back for the results. "Have someone come with you," the doctor said. Something was up.

We suspected Blaine either needed a hernia operation or there was a gallbladder problem, so I was prepared for that. I was at work, so again, Blaine went alone. He put his phone on speaker, and I took the call at work from my cell phone. Standing alone in the junior lunchroom with the door shut, I grabbed a pen and a scrap piece of red construction paper from the counter. I was writing notes as the doctor talked.

"I'm relatively sure there is cancer in Blaine's liver," she said. "Liver cancer rarely originates in the liver."

I can't believe what I'm hearing.

The doctor was explaining the odds of survival of this type of cancer, but my mind could not process what was happening. "We'll need a CT scan to get more information," she said. "There is a slim chance the spots are something other than cancer." She directed her next words to me. "Do you have any questions?" she asked.

I could not process it. "No," I said. I could not think of asking a question that might clarify anything—my mind was a muddle. I knew what I had heard, and I realized the gravity of the situation. A little part of me hoped she had made a terrible mistake. *This was all a misunderstanding, and further tests will show that it is something else. Right?*

I went up to my office in a daze. Tears in my eyes, I told my office manager the news.

Our lives would never be the same. This was the beginning of an uprooting. I left work. I barely remember the drive home. *How did Blaine take the news? Did he hear it the same way I did? If he did, is he okay to drive home?* There was no use phoning him on the way home because the cell service was awful between town and our ranch, so I called him as soon as I got in the door.

I talked to Blaine on the phone as he made the hour-long drive home to our beautiful little ranch along Highway 4. I do not remember our conversation. About ten miles from our house, there was no cell service, and the call dropped. I sat on pins and needles until Blaine drove into the yard. He came up the stairs into the kitchen. I grabbed him and hugged him. *That was the longest ten minutes I've had to wait in my life.*

From there, everything is a blur. We liked to walk together and talk things out. Nature was the best medicine. So, we went out for a walk. There was some beautiful hoarfrost in the trees along our road. I took a selfie of the two of us with the trees in the background. I tried to be calm. But I was panicking. *I can't imagine a life without my husband.* "They do not know us," I said. "They don't know what we're capable of." I believed our love could conquer all.

In January 2021, after a colonoscopy and scope, the doctors diagnosed Blaine with stage 4 colon cancer. His chemotherapy treatments in Saskatoon were to start in February. I finished out the semester at the school, and at the end of January, I took a leave of absence.

"We should move," Blaine said.

At first, I thought that was a terrible idea given the circumstances, but he was right. We would need to be closer to medical practitioners. After over thirty years in education, I would be eligible for my full pension. I said I would like to retire in Maple Creek because it was close to my favorite place in the world, the Cypress Hills.

Blaine agreed. It was closer to the hospital, and our son, Curtise, and his wife, Jennifer, a nurse, lived in Maple Creek. It seemed like a good fit. Blaine loved checking out real estate on the computer, so it seemed fitting he would find our retirement home. He showed me pictures of a beautiful Maple Creek home, and I fell in love with the house and yard. Within a week, we had bought our retirement home. Looking back, what followed was a perfect distraction for me. I was busy going through our things and packing boxes.

The chemotherapy made Blaine so sick he was frequently in and out of hospitals between appointments.

In April, with the help of family and friends, we moved to Maple Creek. I was happy to have Curtise and Jen nearby. Our daughter, Whitney, and her partner, Sheldon, came to visit often, as they were just about ninety minutes away. I started searching for more information about Blaine's condition. Some people suggested Blaine go to a special treatment center. I bought a book called *The Day the Cancer Quit* by Kristie Anne Mah, an author from Alberta who tells the story of how her husband beat pancreatic cancer. The strange thing? I could not bring myself to read the entire book. The story was amazing. I was afraid of not being able to follow through with Mah's suggestions. I knew neither Blaine nor his dieticians would be on board with some of the dietary suggestions. In the book, Mah and her husband traveled to Europe for his treatments and they attended a Joe Dispenza Advanced Meditation Workshop in Cancun, where her husband was chosen for a special group healing. COVID-19 restrictions and Blaine's condition made travel impossible, so that was out.

Mah's book came with a companion gratitude journal. As a school administrator, I had done a lot of research on the benefits of building a gratitude practice into your day, and it had been part of our professional development program at the school. The research on gratitude had been so impressive, I had ordered gratitude journals for the staff and added a gratitude section to our meetings.

So, I understood the importance of a gratitude practice. On May 28, I put my first entry into that journal. That started a daily habit. Every evening before I went to sleep, I wrote in the journal three things I felt grateful for, my favorite moment of the day, and how I had shared kindness that day. This practice was life-changing for me. I never missed a day. In fact, I looked forward to that practice every night. I know without a doubt it helped me change my mindset before I went to sleep at night and helped me get the rest I needed.

Shortly after we moved into our new Maple Creek home, my soon-to-become son-in-law, Sheldon Booth, was diagnosed with lymphoma. I could not process it. I had reached a saturation point. As a safety mechanism, my energy became disconnected from the present moment. In the energy medicine world, we might refer to this as "being ungrounded." I was running on autopilot.

In times of overwhelming challenge, we human beings have inner resilience. When a situation is incomprehensible, we can, at best, function enough to get by day to day. Until such time as we can wrap our heads around upsetting events and make peace with them, we are merely surviving.

In June, I retired from my position at the school. The summer was a barrage of appointments, chemotherapy, and doing everything possible to help Blaine and Sheldon through what felt like a nightmare. On July 2, they took their chemotherapy sessions together in the hospital in Swift Current, Saskatchewan. That experience created a deep bond between them. They had each other in this scary and painful circumstance.

My gratitude practice was helping me be mindful of the beauty in each day. I reflected on my gratitude journal entry from the day they began chemotherapy together. I had written:

> *I was grateful Whitney and I got to spend the morning together. I got to hold Bentley and Lewis and pet Molly (my kids' fur babies). I am thankful for the air-conditioning. It is unbearably hot outside. The highlight of my day was sitting on Whitney's deck, admiring the lake view. Blaine gave me a big kiss and a hug goodnight tonight.*

That day, my act of kindness had been to purchase a bird feeder for my new next-door neighbor, Joanne, and make a card for her with my Cricut craft machine. I used my Cricut for working on monogrammed cups for Whitney and the bridesmaids to use at her best friend's bachelorette party. I recorded those accomplishments in my gratitude journal too.

Blaine and I did our best to stay positive despite many tough days. Our thirty-fifth wedding anniversary, on July 19, came and went quietly. That day, I wrote in my journal:

> *I am grateful for the fact today is our 35th anniversary. Mom and Dad were with us for the day. Curtise and Jen made us a bagel breakfast brunch. We got calls*

from Whitney and Sheldon, my brother Calvin, and my cousin Jenny, and other written messages. I took the card I made and the bird feeder to Joanne and she gave me lettuce and onions from her garden.

Although I had wanted to spend more time in Cypress Hills that summer, we stayed mostly in Maple Creek. Blaine felt more at ease in the comfort of our home. Under the circumstances, Cypress Hills, my go-to place for solace, was neither accessible nor comfortable.

August brought more sadness. We put our faithful, beautiful, Australian shepherd and collie cross pup, Patches, to rest. He, too, had a tumor in his colon. I remember picking up Patches as a puppy. When I held him for the first time, he rested his head on my shoulder. We knew then we were going to take him home, and he would be part of our family. Patches had been with us on the ranch for fourteen years. He was Blaine's dog especially, spending most of his time working cattle and following Blaine faithfully wherever he went on the ranch. The move to town was hard on him. He was not used to town life. He kept me busy taking him for walks around the neighborhood and he kept Blaine company when I was doing the daily house chores. He truly was a service dog, and he helped us through difficult times. The day Patches was scheduled to go to the vet to be put to rest, our friend Joan Tremblay from Nanaimo was doing a healing session with Blaine on Facetime. "Put the phone camera on Patches," she said, "and I will take messages from him." I switched the phone's view so Joan could see Patches. "He is ready to go," she said. "He sees your pain and plans to take as much of that pain with him as he can when he leaves this earth."

I lay on the floor alone with Patches, tears running down my face, thanking him for all the years he loved us unconditionally through our busy lives. He truly was heaven sent. Little did I know that Patches would teach me how to sit with my pain. It was like his last service to me was to prepare me for what was to come. I could not bear to take Patches to the vet, so Curtise, Whitney, and Sheldon went together and kept him company. They said Patches was chill in the waiting room, sleeping while they were getting him ready. It was like he knew—like he wanted to go. I thank my children for being with Patches in his final moments. They stayed with him until the very end. Patches was and is so loved.

The Pain of Initial Grief

I did not know it, but the day the doctor diagnosed Blaine, I started grieving. Not because I believed he would die; I was hanging on to hope that he would survive. I mourned the life we had before these worries. Blaine was fighting for his life, and, over time, I lost the man I knew to the disease. He was not the happy, teasing, joking Blaine I used to know. He was focused on what was ahead, doing the best he could to survive day to day. I understood that.

Blaine was grieving too. But he showed no sadness or anger and stayed positive. Even though the chemotherapy was ruthless, and it took its toll, Blaine kept in touch with family and friends by phone. Slowly, the chemotherapy and cancer took his voice, his focus, and his interest in the life going on around him. He lost so much weight, I barely recognized him.

Blaine and I both felt a sense of loss for the life we had. We did our best to imagine a future. We prayed. We meditated. We had worked through enormous challenges together before, and we would work through this too. Our discussions were often about him getting a Mustang. He had always wanted one. It never happened. Blaine also wanted us to take a trip across Canada in a motorhome. He imagined us stopping at campgrounds and visiting people along the way. "You will make me sandwiches while I drive," he said. He loved food! We made a bargain—if he made it through this ordeal, we would spread the word of hope to whomever we met along the way.

At this point in anticipatory grief, I was going through the motions, just getting through each day. I did not want to feel the pain, and to keep from falling into an emotional tunnel, I kept busy. I did not want to cry in front of Blaine (or anyone else). I wanted to stay strong for him and our family. Blaine did not like to see me cry. He discouraged it—perhaps because if I cried, he might cry too.

As a school principal, as with any leadership position, the goal is to lead while keeping your emotions at bay. Doing otherwise would be unprofessional. So, over the years, I got good at holding back my emotions. Looking back, I can see that all professionals need an outlet in which they can release their emotions outside of their business environment.

Now, here I was, retired, and my world was crashing down around me. It was too much. A couple of times, I fell apart. I blew up like a volcano. Each time, I regretted making a fuss in front of Blaine. He did not need that. Eventually, I vowed I would not let that happen again—and I did not. Often, though, I was on the edge of snapping. I was strong and held it together. I had to. Sometimes, I cried myself to sleep at night, quietly, so Blaine would not hear. Sometimes I had the freedom to cry in the kitchen while I did the dishes. If I could not bear the pain, I allowed myself these tiny releases. I know now that it is helpful when you are grieving to find places and times in which to release these emotions without worry or fear, feeling you are not being strong or that you are being inconsiderate.

Caregivers

One thing I found difficult was my role as a caretaker. We were losing ground with Blaine's health, and I wanted him to try harder. "Okay, Blaine. Want to get up and take a little walk?" I asked. "Can I bring you something to eat?" I never thought there would come a day when he could not find his appetite. It was frustrating and overwhelming. I wanted to go for walks with him. We had gotten him a scooter so he could come with me. I have a video of us all walking as a family, and our cat, Lucky, riding on Blaine's lap on the scooter. These moments were precious. They were also few. Often, he did not feel good enough to do any of it. I searched in desperation for anything that might help him. I watched so many summits and podcasts, it would make your head spin. My two master's degrees gave me research skills, and I was diligent. I scoured the web. When I was not scrolling, I was reading books. If I did enough research, I believed I would find what we needed to beat this terrible disease. I read about miracle cures and thought that if I kept looking, I would find one for Blaine. It gave me hope to think that if I did my research properly, he could beat this cancer.

There was so much conflicting information about treatments. I followed a Facebook page and learned about all the successful and unsuccessful stories and all the ways people were trying desperately to help heal their loved ones with cancer. In the end, it became overwhelming. *What should we believe?* We went to a naturopath, and she made helpful, logical suggestions, but medical staff and pharmacists shot them down. *What should I do? Whom should I listen to?* The chemotherapy treatments seemed to be killing Blaine.

Are they helping enough to make it worth the suffering? Should we go ahead with the homeopathic suggestions and not tell the doctor? What if that causes more complications? Would a little curcumin really thin his blood so much it will be harmful? Should we cut out the sugar in his diet? What about when he has no appetite, or when nothing except ice cream tastes good? Is it better to eat ice cream with the sugar than nothing at all?

This was one of the worst parts of being a caregiver. Jen is a nurse, and with her help, I organized Blaine's medication and read the directions and gave him his medicines on time. *But is this all I can do? Will I just sit and watch this happen? There must be more.* I found myself wishing we lived in a world where traditional Western medicine could be more open to working with natural medicine. It seemed to me if we could all pool our resources and share what we know to be true collectively, we would be better off. Working together, we could reinvent healing.

As a caretaker, I discovered a few helpful things. One was what author and energy healing practitioner Donna Eden refers to as the DER (Daily Energy Routine). You can find the official routine on YouTube with Donna. The URL is included in the Exercises at the end of this chapter. This simple routine helped me release stuck emotions. I did Donna's DER each time I felt stressed or overwhelmed—sometimes multiple times a day. It was something I could do, something I could control, and each time I did it, I felt better because it helped to get the suppressed emotion moving again. My favorite technique was Donna's Triple Warmer Smoothie. I used it for both myself and Blaine every day. I ran my hands from his eyes and forehead around his ears, down his neck, over his shoulders, and onto his heart. It is used to calm the fight, flight, or freeze response and helps calm the nervous system. You can find that technique in the Exercises as well. I bought Donna's book, followed her teachings, and used what I had learned to help Blaine. Energy medicine techniques such as grounding, centering, and balancing the body's energy systems can help us all become more present. This becomes increasingly important when your life is filled with the challenge of caregiving for someone you love.

Important wisdom I can share is to spend as much time as you can in the present moment with your loved one. Try sitting with them. Feel into their presence. I see now that searching the internet for remedies and scrolling through my phone for answers was a distraction. I needed to be present with Blaine and with my emotions. All the answers I sought were inside me. What does that mean? Our higher selves will give us all the information we need if we ask. It is not like the answers necessarily come instantly, or even that the answers will just come to us. But we have to be reasonable about the amount of time we spend looking for answers.

There is a divine plan. I have found that once we take the time to ask, then we must trust that, no matter what happens, we will be okay. It is not easy, but if we have faith in our higher selves and focus on each day, moment by moment, we can get through these challenging times.

All my research put pressure on me: *Find the cure before time runs out!* I worried. I felt inadequate. Nothing worked. I could not think of anything beyond Blaine's survival. Now, looking back, had I known he would leave this world so soon, I would have spent more time holding his hand, looking into his eyes, and being in his presence. I am not saying, "Give up hope." I am saying, "Surrender to whatever you face each day. Take time to embrace each day and each moment as it comes."

Caregivers need to find a balance between spending time with their loved one and doing things to help themselves mentally, emotionally, and physically. We are all different. We are all in unique situations. It is not a one-size-fits-all solution. Taking time to go into our heart space and sit in the stillness helps. It does not have to be a special meditation. Setting a timer for a few minutes and just sitting still and breathing can do a great service to you and everyone around you. I found The Wonder Method by Alain Herriot easy to do and helpful. When you sit with the energy, have no expectations. Just breathe. You can also ask yourself, "What do I need in this moment to feel better?" This time is for you.

We forget that in order to be in a space where we can help, we need to look after ourselves. I like the analogy that we can fill our cup until it overflows to those around us. We feed others from our saucer. Even if you think you are okay, it never hurts to check in with yourself—what else can you do to help fill your cup? Being still is important. Often, we ignore our body signals. We push away simple things like hydration and rest. If we can stay on top of those things, they will not become something much worse. I cannot stress how important it is to stay in touch with your own needs.

I will never regret how I looked after Blaine over those months. I did the best I could with what I knew. I put my heart and soul into making him comfortable. It was my great honor to serve him. "Til death do us part" was more than just a saying to me. It was a commitment, and I fulfilled it. It was my gift to the man who gave me so much love and support over all those years. He did more for me than I could ever express. Caregiving is a truly sacred act that deserves reverence.

Journal Exercise:

- What is your story? It can be very therapeutic to tell your story. I was fortunate to have opportunities to tell my story on podcasts, in my blog posts, and in other ways many times. Each time I told the story, I internalized it. I recommend writing your story. You do not have to share it with anyone, but if you do, it has the potential to help someone else.

Energy Routines:

- Try the following exercises as ways to help you release blocked energy. As you do each exercise, be intentional. Take your time. Once you have learned the procedure, you can use it over and over. The whole regimen will only take a few minutes to do, and you will quickly discover which parts of the pattern are most helpful for you. Choose to do those particular parts of the routine more often if needed.
  - Daily Energy Routine[5]
  - Triple Warmer Smoothie[6]

Chapter 3

Facing the Worst

Praying for a Miracle

For many years, oracle cards have captivated me, offering me comfort and guidance as I pull them and read their messages. Blaine usually found comfort in the cards, but as his cancer progressed, he had less interest in anything. During the transition from summer to fall, I wanted to receive a direct message from God or my guides. I had heard energy healers talk about their guides' messages. *Why aren't I getting any of these messages or guidance?* I tried dowsing. I had little experience and did not trust the answers I was getting. *What should I ask?* I did not want to the answer to disappoint me. I was too emotionally involved to be neutral, but I believed someone out there wanted to communicate with me. I decided to pray for help—to God, to the angels, and to my guides—and I would listen to what they had to say. I kept my mind open.

One morning, I awoke with a message in my mind. This was the first message I had received that was specific and clear. The message included the words, "read *A New Earth*" and "a conversation with Rita." I ordered *A New Earth* by spiritual teacher Eckhart Tolle and received it on September 3. Each time I read the book, I found guidance in its pages. As far as "a conversation with Rita," I could not find a single reference to that. Only after several months did I realize the true meaning of that message.

Sheldon completed his chemo treatments in September, and we rejoiced—he had a clean scan! Whitney arranged a gathering in the parking lot of the hospital for people to cheer as Sheldon finished his last treatment. Blaine was too sick to go. I watched the video of the event and was so happy and relieved.

Blaine's chemo treatments, on the other hand, were not working as expected, and we had to go to Saskatoon for a different type of treatment. Unfortunately, after that treatment, Blaine contracted COVID-19. He got through it surprisingly well, but it did not do him any service. It took time, but when his blood counts came back up, the oncologist said he could take another treatment.

Blaine wanted to go. "It might help with my pain," he said. I was not convinced he was strong enough, but I wheeled him up to the second floor of the hospital and dropped him off at the treatment center.

The nurse could see I was concerned. "We'll check all his vitals before we do the treatment," she assured me.

After that treatment, his medical care team called. "We'll set up a call with palliative care," they said, "and we'll prescribe some medication to make him comfortable." That call scared me so much.

I remember going to the garage at home and talking to Joan on the phone. I was crying, "Blaine is everything to me. He is my rock. He is the one that always supported me. I would not be who I am without him. How can I possibly live without him?" She was amazing. She listened to me while I cried. It was the first time I had really opened up to anyone about how I felt. She told me she was not giving up hope. I appreciated her saying that. It was hope that kept me going. The release of emotion was freeing.

I do not know how long I was gone. When I returned to our bedroom, Blaine had been waiting for me. I am sure he could see I had been crying. He never mentioned it. I kept Blaine at home until the day before he died. Over the course of ten months, I helped him up to the bathroom and back into bed. I put essential oils on his feet. I rubbed his back. I gave him energy healing sessions several times a day, and he had energy healing sessions from two other healers. These sessions kept him comfortable enough that he could get by just with Tylenol. I did not realize until much later how incredible and miraculous that was.

Even after his medical team called with the news that Blaine was to go into palliative care, Blaine and I were still hoping and praying for a miracle. We had not given up, although I was starting to realize: *He might not make it.*

The day before Blaine passed, on October 25, the oncologist (whom we had never met in person because we always communicated on the phone) called. He did not have good news. He told us to get our affairs in order.

I called Jen. "Will you come and visit Blaine this morning?" I knew that Jen's nursing skills would be helpful.

Blaine had a rough night. He was confused and in and out of consciousness. Jen believed we had a day or two before he passed. I agreed. Somehow, between what the oncologist had said and what my intuition was saying, I knew she was right. The reaction I had, upon reflection, appeared to be (again) auto-pilot mode. To me, it is like a survival setting that kicks in when we need it most.

Jen and I called Whitney. Whitney had wanted to get married with her dad present, so she set up a wedding for that afternoon with a marriage commissioner. I called the flower shop, and they put a bouquet together and delivered it to the house. Whitney had already bought her dress. I told Blaine, "Whitney and Sheldon are getting married today."

He said, "I won't be able to walk her down the aisle." I said, "It is okay. She doesn't expect you to. She only wants you to be here."

When I think about this, it breaks my heart in two. There is nothing Blaine would have loved more than to have walked his daughter down the aisle. Whitney married Sheldon in our new home, in our bedroom, where Blaine could see and hear the service and be as comfortable as possible. Somehow, perhaps by a miracle, Blaine clapped his hands over his head when Sheldon and Whitney were proclaimed husband and wife.

When the wedding was over, and the marriage commissioner was leaving, Blaine was trying to speak. He seemed agitated and kept repeating a word over and over. After many attempts, Curtise figured out he was saying "tip"—he wanted to ensure we had tipped the commissioner for coming on short notice. This is who Blaine was: a kind, generous, thoughtful guy, and a blessing as a husband and father. That same afternoon Curtise and Jennifer announced that they were expecting a baby. Blaine was able to congratulate them. I know he would have been a wonderful grandfather.

Shortly after the wedding, we called the ambulance. The paramedics took Blaine to the hospital. I rode with the kids to the hospital to see him. The nurses gave us a beautiful corner room, big enough for the kids and me to sit around comfortably. I stayed with Blaine overnight, sleeping in another bed in the room. I slept (can you believe it?). I suppose after a day like I had just had, it might have been more like I had passed out! When I woke early the next morning, I went to his bedside. He was unresponsive. I called the kids. "Come now," I told them.

When the kids arrived, we all said our goodbyes. You could tell that Blaine, as weak as he was, was saying goodbye too. It was so difficult to watch Whitney and Curtise say goodbye to their dad. I was filled with such love. I felt so much gratitude for all the kids. Blaine loved his kids, and I know that when Sheldon and Jen came along, he felt like he had gained two more children. He was (and still is) so proud of them. I was so proud of them for their strength and courage. There are no words to express how blessed we are.

I remember telling Blaine, "It's okay if you have to leave. We'll be okay. Our kids are strong, just like you." I used the Donna Eden Triple Warmer Smoothie energy healing technique that I had done with Blaine so many times every day for so many months. I could not think of anything else to do. I learned through a private channeling session that, in fact, this helped him to pass gently.

The nurses came in. "We'll change Blaine's bed to an airbed, to make him more comfortable," they said. The kids thought it was a good chance to let their dogs out of Curtise and Jenn's house for a bit. "You can take a short walk," the nurses told me.

I messaged our friend Joan and updated her on what was happening. When I returned to Blaine's room, I knew he had passed. The nurse went for a stethoscope and confirmed it. I felt myself go weak. This beautiful nurse came running from the other side of the bed and gave me the most compassionate, much-needed hug. I will never forget it. I cannot thank her enough.

I called Whitney, and the nurse called Curtise. They came back to the hospital. *What do I do next?* I was a widow—I would have to figure this one out without Blaine. Walking out of the hospital with my kids was a feeling I will never forget. Somehow it felt surreal knowing in that moment everything had changed. I got into the truck with Curtise, and we drove back to my house. I remember him saying to me that I had done a good job of looking after Dad. It was exactly what I needed to hear.

When I think about the upheaval our family underwent in that year, I shake my head in disbelief. Retiring and moving would be enough of a shock to a person's system. I could look forward to being a grandma, but without a grandpa to share it with. *How am I supposed to feel about that? How am I supposed to cope?* It was overwhelming. Somehow, I made it through. There were days where I wanted to crawl into a hole and never come out. I questioned my sanity. I questioned every belief I have ever had, including my own existence. Somehow, deep inside, I knew I had to find a way to continue on for myself and my family.

Fight, Flight, and Freeze

Grief affects our nervous system. Understanding our reaction to grief requires understanding how our human brain and nervous system keep us safe. When our mind perceives danger, usually we react in one of three ways. One way is to fight. We get angry, frustrated, or irritated. The next way is flight, whereby we get anxious, worried, or afraid. We want to run. Alternatively, we may freeze. We are tired, numb, or hopeless, or we despair. When we freeze, we disengage.

I watched a video on TikTok of a fellow encountering a cougar and her cub on a hiking path. The cougar follows the man. His camera is recording the cougar's pursuit as the man backs up on a stony path. The man's autonomic nervous system kicks in—he backs up quickly (flight). He tries to make himself big to scare the cougar off and roars back at it (fight). The cougar turns and goes back to her cub. The man is safe.

Had the cougar pounced, the man's nervous system would have gone into freeze mode. In that case, his best chance of survival would have been to lie still and hope the cougar would lose interest. When we go into freeze mode, the vagus nerve shuts off our ability to feel, so we lay still, immobilized.

We do not control when the autonomic nervous system takes over and our body gets ready for the fight, flight, or freeze response. It does it before we can even think. Our autonomic nervous system can react to a significant loss as a threat, just as it would react to a cougar attack. To our mind, a threat is a threat. Throughout the days following a loss, events and memories can activate us, and the fight, flight, or freeze response can kick in. It can be uncomfortable. We can withdraw from activities we used to love, use drugs or alcohol, or fight with family or friends.

There is more and more research and information now on the vagus nerve, which is a major component of the autonomic nervous system. The relationship between the autonomic nervous system and the vagus nerve is important for regulating many vital bodily functions and maintaining overall health and well-being such as heart rate, digestion, and respiratory rate. It can be instrumental in helping us calm our system when we are in an automatic response. Breathwork, meditation, and vocalization can influence the nervous system. These can regulate the impact of stress on the body naturally. Donna Eden provides simple and effective techniques for calming the fight, flight, or freeze response and for calming the vagus nerve. Getting emotional help from a therapist, counselor, or coach can also help us find ways to relieve these responses.

The Support of Family and Friends

After Blaine's passing, there was a lot to do. I occupied my mind by taking care of arrangements, and I was fortunate to have the support of my family and friends throughout these challenging tasks. I have always been a natural introvert. I wanted my alone time when I was hurting, and yet in this time of deep initial grief, I needed people around me. I could feel the energetic support. It was as if the grief was shared somehow. I was surprised at the strength it provided me to do what I needed to get done.

As soon as he heard the news, my brother, Calvin, flew in from Campbell River. My family had moved to Vancouver Island after Blaine and I were married, so Calvin and I have had a long-distance relationship for years. I was so happy to see him. He is the practical, logical guy I needed to help me through the decision-making process. It is uncanny—

Curtise has developed so many mannerisms that are similar to Calvin's even though they have not spent a lot of time together. They may both be unaware of those innate superpowers that helped me stay clear and focused on the tasks in front of me!

All energy healers talk about the balance between masculine and feminine energies, and I could see that balance was happening for me. I was balancing the masculine, logical, methodical process of getting things arranged for Blaine's celebration of life with the feminine energy of heartfelt emotion and creating a celebration that would help us all to honor him. I worked on the eulogy, and that was healing for me. Calvin agreed to read it. I did not know it then and did not expect that writing would be the creative act I needed to express my grief. I also worked on the script for the graveside service, which would be read by the funeral director.

My mom and dad were in Arizona visiting my Aunt Sharon and Uncle Don, who have a place in Mesa they visit in the winter months. Mom and Dad had wondered whether they should go to Arizona. But at the time, Blaine had been stable and was doing fine, and he had told them, "Go. Enjoy yourselves." How quickly things can change. They had to do a COVID-19 test before flying back, resulting in a couple of days' delay. Meanwhile, Blaine's family and friends took great care of me. I was never alone or unsupported. Despite now being in Maple Creek, over two hours away from Val Marie, I received support from the community through texts, calls, and visits. I will never forget this and am deeply thankful.

Curtise, Whitney, and I went to the funeral home together. I was so grateful for their support. I admire and appreciate the knowledge and patience of the people in the funeral home. In a society that does not discuss grief, they are so important. The bereaved can barely get out of bed, yet they must make big decisions about how to honor a person they love. Fortunately, the COVID-19 restrictions had been lifted, and, with few restrictions, we could hold the event in the town hall in Val Marie. I felt having a gathering back home was crucial since Blaine could not have visitors while he was sick, and we had left without saying goodbye properly to our community of thirty-five years. Blaine had lived there his entire life. He was well-known, loved, and adored. People wanted to honor him and say goodbye.

We did not need a church, a minister, or a priest for Blaine's service because his church was the land he grew up on. God was all around him: The prairie grasses, the animals, the gentle creek flowing through the ranch land, and the beautiful prairie sky were his home. This was the sacred place where he had asked all the big questions and found his answers.

My friend Judy sat with me while we picked out what pictures to use in the slide show she put together for the celebration of life. Blaine's cousin Jim emceed the event and did a fitting tribute. My niece Ashlee told a heartwarming story. People from town set up the tables and put cans of Coke on them. That is the beautiful thing about living in a small town—everyone knew Blaine loved a good, cold can of Coke. It was a tribute to him.

The kids and I decided we would split Blaine's ashes. We would bury half next to his parents in the Val Marie cemetery, and the other half we would spread in the Cypress Hills where we spent our summers. When we were at the funeral home, Whitney spotted a monument that had a ranch feel to it. It was perfect. I was glad she pointed it out because later, it helped make another hard task easier.

Response to Initial Grief

Once the celebration of life was over, and family and friends went on with their lives, I found the days quieter. Mom stayed with me for a month, which helped me transition from living without Blaine to living alone. There are many common responses to loss, and I experienced them all: numbness; impulsivity; lack of direction, focus, and optimism; and overwhelm. Some people disconnect from their family and friends and lose interest in taking care of themselves physically. Many people respond by trying to flee from or numb the emotion by watching TV, using alcohol and/or drugs, eating, or getting busy.

Getting busy was my go-to. My days were filled with errands. I paid the bills, organized the finances, and did everyday chores like cleaning and cooking. I did not feel like watching TV; that was something Blaine had done. I had watched whatever he had on and if I did not like it, I did something else. I spent time on my phone, searching for information. I was looking for anything that would help me in my grief. I explored the world of spiritual experts and healers. I purchased online courses about ancestral healing, shamanism, and mediumship. I listened to Eckhart Tolle and his partner, Kim Eng. I booked sessions with healers. I branched out and found resources, like free meditations or energy activations, which are techniques that bring your body back into energetic balance. I attended webinars and masterclasses on subjects like spirituality, healing, and grief. I read books about grief. I was busy, and I was thinking about things I might do to keep myself busy in the future.

I decided to take up macrame and ordered the materials. My cousin Holly does a beautiful job of making these, and she helped me get everything I needed. I tried making a macrame snowflake. It was floppy and uneven and certainly did not replicate, by any means, the beauty and perfection of a snowflake. I have not looked at macrame since. I signed up for energy healing classes. I went to the curling rink and curled a few games with Blaine's delivery stick. I thought about places I could travel to, like out to Mom and Dad's in Campbell River, or to see Sharon and Don in Arizona. Both places were much warmer in the winter than Saskatchewan, so it seemed like a good plan. All this thinking and doing was a great distraction. I did not want to feel. It was not a bad thing—initial grief can be overwhelming, and had I not kept busy, it may have been too much for me. However, you cannot keep that pace up long term. Eventually, you have to slow down, take the time, and face the emotions.

My biggest goal was to be strong and positive. There are reasons for this. We are told to stay strong, and when we are busy and out and about doing things, friends and family praise us for doing well. It might feel like a nice compliment, and maybe we are doing well in spite of being in a deep state of grief. But I can assure you, at this stage, I was far from doing well. I do not think we get through this period of initial grief without feeling like we are falling apart. It feels like the rug has been pulled out from underneath us.

Even if we can hold up during the day, the nights are hard. We miss our person so much. It is devastating. I look back at my journal entries for the months after Blaine passed, and my journal is filled with everything I had done each day *and* how I missed Blaine. I filled my days with activities we used to do together. Eating out, going to a movie, curling, sitting in the back yard, heading to my favorite camping spot—it was all challenging. Everything we do after we lose a loved one has the potential to activate sadness. Each time the sadness came up, I did my best to swallow it. Sheldon and Whitney were planning a traditional wedding celebration for the following summer, and Curtise and Jen were expecting their baby in June. I needed to be the mom they deserved to have, and I decided I would be strong for them. Now, looking back, I realize that a strong mom would not be afraid to show emotion in front of her kids.

There were times I pushed through tears. Once, for example, I went in person to pay the car insurance, something Blaine usually looked after, so it made sense it would be an emotional event. There I was, in a new town where I did not know anyone—and it made me sad and angry he was not here to do it. It was probably awkward for the poor fellow on the other end of the desk seeing the tears I was trying to hold back. *What should I do about Blaine's name on the insurance policies?* I was determined to fight through and get it all taken care of. I could feel Blaine's presence, letting me know he was supporting me and guiding me. I knew he would be pleased I was taking care of things. As difficult as it was, I walked out of that building feeling proud and relieved I had made it through something so hard.

This set the stage for my approach moving forward. Some people rip off the Band-Aid slowly and gently. Some people rip it off quickly and get it over with. I am more of a get-it-over-with person, so I approached a lot of things with the thought, *Well, I have to get this done.* I equate it to jumping into a pool, knowing full well it could be cold, and facing the consequences. I had a running list of tasks, and each day I tackled something on the list. I sucked it up and plowed through, but as the months went on, I could not keep up the pace. I knew I was going to need help. It was getting increasingly difficult to put on a brave face every day with all the emotions that just kept on coming.

Exercises:
A higher vagal tone indicates that the body will return to a state of relaxation more quickly after experiencing stress.

We can do some simple exercises to increase the tone of the vagus nerve:

1. Place your index finger behind the bottom back of your ear. Your fingertips will land in the valley behind your ear. Gently massage that part of your ear and behind your ear where it attaches to your head. Breathe.

2. Practice singing, humming, or chanting. The vagus nerve controls the muscles in the voice box. When you sing, hum, or chant, you create vibrations that automatically stimulate the muscles in the throat that communicate with the vagus nerve. When I was having anxiety attacks, I hummed or sang and this calmed my system. Important: You just have to make noise. There is no need to be "on tune" or sound nice.

Calls to Action:

1. Join a support group. Joining a support group can be incredibly helpful. Here are a few benefits:

    a. Understanding and Validation: Being in a support group allows you to connect with others who are going through similar experiences. Having your grief acknowledged in this way is very important for your healing.

    b. Emotional Support: Support groups provide a safe, comforting space for you to express your feelings and emotions.

    c. Coping Strategies and Tools: A good support group will not only give you an opportunity to express what you are going through but will provide practical coping strategies and tools to help guide you through the grieving process.

    d. Normalization of the Grieving Process: Through listening to others, you will find that there is a wide range of emotions and experiences associated with loss. You will discover that your reactions are valid and part of the natural grieving process.

e. Community Building: Support groups offer the opportunity to build connections and form meaningful relationships with others who resonate with you. These new friendships can extend beyond the group meetings, providing a network of support and understanding.

2. Sign up for the Awaken Your Soul's Journey Group Get Together on Zoom. URL: https://subscribepage.io/XhjDUf

   ○ We have a wonderful community that meets about every ten days. You are welcome to join in anytime you are ready. A support group is not a substitute for (but is a perfect complement to) having a coach, therapist, or counselor. Sign up for my newsletter at www.healingenergy.world to get more information about the group.

PART II

Heart Healing and Opening

Chapter 4

Walking Through the Emotion of Grief

Introduction

In this section, I provide examples of things that helped me open myself up to healing and restoration. When we experience loss, we feel vulnerable and afraid, and it is natural for us to contract. Our hearts close. The first thing I had to learn was to reopen my heart. I did this with the help of energy healing. I learned about what was happening in my brain, about my emotions, how to process them, and how to let go and surrender. I deepened my spiritual connection, realized there is more to me than what I had originally understood, and started to feel better. It was all part of my grief process and my journey to finding meaning.

Energy Healing for Grief

Since I was young, spirituality and things beyond this physical world have intrigued me. Back then, my imagination ran wild. Once, I believed I was a penguin. For a while, I rode an imaginary horse, even tying it up to make sure it was there for me the next day. When we are young, our imaginations are free. As we grow older, we see them as unimportant. Our imaginative ideas are disregarded as not credible. As I grew older, my imagination faded, but my interest in what I could feel but not see was still strong. In my teens, I found a book on the sixth sense in our school library and read it, fascinated.

Over the years, I developed an interest in energy healing. I gained firsthand experience with energy healing when Curtise was about four years old. He was born with a condition called Hirschprung's disease. When ganglion cells in the colon fail to develop correctly, it can cause constipation because of delayed stool progression. This would constipate my little boy so badly his stomach would bloat, and food would back up in his esophagus. He would try to grunt, and often the food choked him. As a new mother, it was terribly frightening. A diagnosis took months. There were frequent hospital visits and anxious days and nights. Curtise had surgery to correct the problem when he was about a year old, and it helped somewhat. However, by the time he was four, he was still constipated, and I could not potty train him. I was worried about him being able to attend school. A friend suggested I go see a healer named Roxene Harris.

She called herself a "metaphysical healer." She lived a three-and-a-half-hour drive away in Regina, Saskatchewan.

On the way to the appointment, Blaine kept saying, "I can't believe we are driving all this way to see a witch!" He did not believe in this hocus pocus. I insisted. I was at my rope's end. We needed to try something.

When we got to the Roxene's door, she opened it and greeted us with, "And just so you know, I am not a witch." That sent Blaine into a state of panic. Worried she could read his mind, he tried to shut off his thoughts while we were there.

It excited me to think of what Roxene might do to help our son. We went for three sessions with her, and in between sessions she called and talked to Curtise on the phone to keep the healing energy moving. Eventually, Roxene came to Val Marie to do workshops, and I continued to take Curtise to her. In the end, he healed completely. There are many stories about ways Roxene helped members of my family and our friends. People drove from miles around to get energy healing sessions with her.

Roxene told me a story about a man she had worked with who had cancer. She could not heal him, but she helped him with his symptoms. I wondered, *How did she know she could not heal him? Why are some people healed and some not? What part of us is so elusive? Will I ever have these types of gifts? What is this energy that is so much bigger and more powerful than our human self can imagine?*

At a day-long workshop, Roxene spent a few hours teaching me about energy healing—it was a kind of activation or attunement into energy healing. I drove home feeling a love I had never felt before. I wanted it to stay forever. This intrigued me, and for the next thirty years, I dabbled in energy healing. I played with the energy and practiced with family and friends. *Could I ever be a healer like*

Roxene? I wanted to learn more. I lost contact with Roxene but continued to study. I read books that delved deeper into our spiritual life and purpose here on earth.

Mom had a friend, Joan Tremblay, who did energy healing. Joan worked with the late Dr. Wayne Dyer. She is an amazing healer who acquired her gifts suddenly. It is an extraordinary story. I developed fibroids, and in addition to seeing my physician, I saw a naturopath and had long-distance healings with Joan. The process of being referred to a specialist for this took several months. By the time I got in to see a surgeon, I no longer needed surgery. I was pleasantly surprised, and so was my doctor. So, when Blaine received his cancer diagnosis, it seemed natural to call Joan to help us out.

We did sessions with Joan on FaceTime. I felt Blaine was getting the help he needed physically and emotionally, and I was benefiting from being in the healing energy as well. Just the fact that he got her support and a reprieve from his painful symptoms was a relief. In the beginning, I recorded the sessions, and later I wrote notes as I listened to each session. Writing helped me to process more than listening did—and it gave my anxious body something to do. I looked forward to being in that comforting space and feeling the expansiveness of the healing energy.

I stumbled upon an online summit and found another healer with whom I resonated, Ana Coeur. I jumped into a free healing session she offered on Zoom. There were about a dozen of us in that call. Ana did a quick session with each of us, and in the few minutes she worked with me, she helped me so much. I came away feeling light and peaceful. She said she could help Blaine and me, and I knew it was true. It made a big difference to me—I could breathe again—and I knew that even if it provided only hope, working with her would be immensely helpful. During her session with Blaine, she shared Alain Herriot's Wonder Method with me. I started classes with him and applied what I had learned to both Blaine and myself.

I was angry with God that Blaine had not healed. *Where was our miracle? Why, when we prayed and stayed positive, did my husband die so soon?* Understanding the larger picture was challenging. But now I know there are no clear answers, and everyone has their own beliefs about why one person might heal and another might not. Perhaps overall health, the mindset of the individual, or their spiritual beliefs come into play. Multiple evidential mediums have told me we all have predetermined agreements and life plans for our experiences on earth, and I believe Blaine and I had a soul agreement. Blaine's death pushed me onto a trajectory I could have never imagined. *Was this always part of the plan? I cannot change what happened, but I can choose how to move forward. If this is the plan, then I had best not waste the opportunity.*

I have become more curious about what my future might be and what I might discover through this journey. Blaine's circumstances magnified my motivation to learn more about energy healing. Besides taking Levels 1 and 2 of the Wonder Method, I took classes from Donna Eden. I purchased her Energy Healing Kit and listened to her YouTube videos. I used the techniques that applied to Blaine's situation. Donna's work is extensive and practical, and her exercises are easy to implement into a daily routine. I was learning constantly, trying different things to help Blaine. Working with energy to help Blaine was something I could do, and I did sessions with him whenever he asked, sometimes more than once a day. He said they helped, and often, they put him to sleep. I enhanced the sessions with crystals or essential oils as I felt was necessary.

My mother, Elaine, became an EFT Practitioner. EFT stands for Emotional Freedom Technique. It is a form of energy psychology, also referred to as "tapping." You tap on specific acupressure points on your body while focusing on the issue that is troubling you. The scripts you find in the Exercises within this book were created by my mother. EFT helps balance the body's energy system and releases emotional blockages. I interviewed and follow several EFT practitioners. I keep tapping as one of the tools in my toolbox I can use when I am feeling I need a release.

One day I was listening to an online summit, and I came across another healer named Cathleena Hailey. In the late summer, I had been listening to an interview with her and something inside told me, "Book a session with her for Blaine." I could not get an appointment until November, so I booked it, and then I forgot about it. When the time for the appointment was near, I received an email notification, and since the session was paid for, and Blaine was gone, I took the appointment for myself. The session I had with Cathleena was referred to as a Frequency Adjustment with Activation of Crystallin DNA. I had no idea what that was, and I did not need to. I was amazed by how I felt after the session. Through her activation, Cathleena helped me release the dense energies of the emotions I felt. She connected with Blaine, gave some great evidence that she was indeed communicating with him, and confirmed that he was doing well on the other side. Cathleena also brought up my intention to travel to Sedona. I had been thinking of traveling to Sedona because I heard about the energy vortices from my Aunt Sharon. These vortices are believed to be areas of concentrated energy that can have a profound effect on individuals who visit them. People report feeling a sense of peace, clarity, and spiritual connection when they visit Sedona. I was curious. Without knowing my interest, Cathleena validated the thoughts I was having about that trip. I believe I was guided to work with her and that it was part of my plan. I continue to see Cathleena as part of my healing.

Blaine was gone. *What will I do?* It seemed natural to continue my study of energy healing. A six-month course starting in January 2022 with celebrity healer Adrien Blackwell introduced me to new modes of healing. I was certified as a Reiki Master and learned the basics of shamanic journeying, ancestral healing, and more. I received and practiced healing with my classmates. Adrien, a powerful healer, spent time with me, helping me heal some of the physical symptoms that arose. Strong emotions can manifest as physical symptoms in the body in various ways. I was experiencing digestive issues, fatigue, and low energy because of the overwhelming emotion. Seeing Adrien and other energy healers and consulting a medical professional helped to relieve these symptoms.

Along the way, I saw different energy healers whom I had found online or on social media. I had a sense deep within me if they were a match. Most I met for one session only—they had exactly what I needed when I needed it. I believe these sessions were divinely guided as I followed my heart and aligned with my divine purpose. Each of these healers arrived in my life at the perfect time. I only needed to say yes.

Walking Through Heavy Emotion

To say the emotions that come with grief are strong is an understatement. The pain is gut wrenching, excruciating, and relentless. The intensity of it can throw you into the depths of extreme fear. But you will make it through! There was a point at which I questioned my existence on this earth and anything and everything I had ever believed in. I wanted to crawl out of my skin. I could not stand the pain. I could not see a way out. I knew no one would understand me, and if they did, they would never be able to help me. Miserable and alone, I did not know where to turn. I was mad at God. I was mad at Blaine for leaving me here. Everyone around me was going on with their lives, and even things that gave me joy at one time were clouded with sadness. The waves of grief happened again and again. It was an internal process. I did not go around telling people this because I did not feel comfortable sharing my thoughts or feelings. The only person I might have ever considered sharing these things with was gone.

Until you have suffered a loss this great, you will not understand this pain. The thing is, we all know it must be awful. You just cannot imagine it until you are in the throes of grief.

Recall I talked earlier about people saying you will carry your grief with you for a lifetime. They say, "You'll get used to it," and "It will get easier." Grief counselor and author Dr. Lois Tonkin explains in her article "Growing Around Grief" that grief does not get smaller. We grow around it. She depicts grief as a black ball inside a jar. As time goes on, the little black circle that represents grief stays the same size, but the surrounding jar gets bigger. Some people like this analogy. I did not because the thought of carrying around the little black circle of pain in my jar of life seemed too heavy a burden. However, one day I thought,

Why do we carry that black ball around with us in our jar of life? I picture grief and that little black ball as a

reminder that we get to choose to put the pain away from time to time and enjoy life a little. Why not put that little black ball on the shelf for a bit and give ourselves a break? Sure, we will need to address that black ball. And in the beginning, it will be there a lot. Yet it doesn't have to be there everywhere we go.

Thinking this made me feel lighter. God did not design us to feel the heavy pain of grief for the rest of our lives. I do not buy into the belief that pain is the price of love. Some say when we love someone so much, we must pay this price. This suggests that if we did not feel the pain as much, we never loved them as much. Not true. Something inside me knew there was no way I was going to feel like this for the rest of my life. I kept searching for another message that resonated with my truth. I shudder to think I could have given up.

In my search to feel better, I found an article online by a fellow named Shawn Doyle. Shawn is a learning and development professional who shares the true story of the sudden, tragic death of his wife of thirty-two years, Cindy. In this brief article titled, "4 Ways to Be Happy Again After Losing a Loved One," Shawn shares how he found his way back to happiness. Believe that you will be okay, believe you can survive and thrive, believe you can reinvent your life, and believe you will be okay where there is not an answer. He wrote about his life before he lost his wife, Life Number One, and after she was gone, how he built Life Number Two. The messages of hope in his article were a big turning point for me. We never know which simple message will give us the hope we need, and I am forever grateful to Shawn Doyle and for the divine intervention that led me to read his article. It was a promise of hope for happiness in the future, even though at that moment I felt awful. Shawn made it through his loss, and there was hope that I could do it too. I also read Shawn's book *The Sun Still Rises*, and it inspired me to have found further confirmation that I would be okay.

One day, I was scrolling through Facebook and found a quote from author and podcaster Julie Cluff. It read: "Some say you will grieve for a lifetime. I choose otherwise. I choose the path from hurt to hope to healing every day." Julie wrote the book *Miracles in the Darkness* and is the host of the *Life After Loss Podcast* and the founder of the HOPE Model of Healing. She became my grief coach and helped me understand my emotions and how I could heal. As soon as I met with her, I knew she had exactly what I needed. I signed up for her twelve-week program. We met once a week, and each week I did my homework diligently, trusting fully in the process. I looked forward to our sessions.

Over the course of the next few months, with Julie, Cathleena, and Adrien supporting me, I learned more about myself and how I could process all that stuck emotion. Julie helped me understand what was happening in my mind and my body. Between her coaching and the support I was getting from spiritual study and work my outlook on life improved quickly.

The first thing I learned was that I needed to feel and express the emotions coming up. Grief is an internal process, and mourning expresses it. As I noted earlier, if we suppress our grief and do not express our emotions through mourning, we cannot move the energy of the emotion and we will not feel better.

I started seeing Julie in January of 2022, just over two months after Blaine's passing. I told her the scariest thing for me about working with her was that I might cry. I grew up, as many of us did, believing sadness, anger, and other dark emotions are bad, and the desirable state is to be happy, joyful, and pleasant. I had never felt strong enough to freely cry in front of someone ... anyone ... not even Blaine. Of course, I had been brought to tears in my life, but often I had suppressed it so long, it came as a tsunami. Once the tears started, they were hard to stop. Julie used the analogy that holding these emotions inside is like holding a beach ball under water. You can only hold it down so long—and then it will fly up in your face! I learned to let out a bit of emotion at a time. Letting out the sadness and despair made room for joy and happiness to come in. It made so much sense.

Each time I felt emotion come to the surface, I acknowledged it. I saw sadness coming up and tried to figure out, *What caused it?* If I was in a space to allow it, I would let it up and out. Each of us finds our own way to do this. Crying was my go-to. If I could cry in private, I did that. Crying is healing because the chemical composition in tears helps bring our bodies back to homeostasis. Tears contain a neurotransmitter that acts as a painkiller. Once I realized I could cry and let it all out, and it would not kill me, I was on board. Now I had control over my healing, and I knew it would be beneficial. After that, I never felt guilty about crying, and that is another key. Crying and then feeling shame or guilt about it does not release the pain. It creates more pain. We must be compassionate and understanding with ourselves, just as we would be with a good friend. We must allow ourselves time to mourn.

Writing and Talking to Heal

In addition to crying, I expressed my emotion by writing or talking it out. With encouragement from those supporting me, I got up the nerve to start a blog. I also have had the opportunity to be a monthly columnist for *Your West Central Voice*, a newspaper serving a large area in West Central Saskatchewan. Some of my writing did not see the light of day, but it was all healing for me. You do not have to be a published author to do this. Creative journaling or scribbling is expressive and will allow the energy to move out. Sometimes I talked out loud with God or my guides. Often, I talked to Blaine and told him why I was feeling sad. I talked to Mom on the phone every day. Telling my story out loud or in writing helped to get my thoughts out in the open where I could see, hear, and process them.

Sitting in silence helped me. Sometimes when I was alone and spoke to Blaine, I "heard" comforting words in my mind. *Is that me? Am I making this up? Are these words from beyond the veil?* I never knew for sure, but it did not matter. The words comforted me, and that was enough.

Some people paint; some people draw or dance or cook or make music. Creating something will help you get what you are feeling out where you can see it, feel it, hear it, or even taste it. You are transmuting the emotional energy. You turn the painful emotion into something beautiful.

As I mentioned earlier, many emotions accompany grief. Remember, do not judge yourself. If you are honest and give yourself the compassion you deserve, in time you will feel better.

Journal Exercises:
- Take inventory of the emotions you are feeling right now. What kind of support would most help you at this time? How might you find those who can support you as you work through the intense emotions of grief?
- Consider investing in a grief coach, healer, or other support person to help you in your grief as feels appropriate. How might working with an energy healer or grief coach help you?

Call to Action:

- Develop a Regular Journaling Practice: Writing down your thoughts, feelings, and memories can be a cathartic way to release emotions. Set aside a regular time to journal, allowing yourself to express your emotions freely without judgment or censorship. I chose to write in my journal just before bed. Perhaps you have another time that works better. It does not have to be long. Set a timer for seven minutes and write down anything that comes to mind. If you cannot think of anything, write that. Make scribbles on the page if nothing else. If after seven minutes you feel like continuing, that is great. If not, congratulate yourself for making that commitment to yourself. This is the first step to developing a habit. I am cheering you on. You got this!

Chapter 5

———

Healing Through Emotion

Jealousy

Many of us have been told it is wrong to be jealous, so it can be embarrassing to admit we feel that way. Sometimes we feel ashamed about our feelings and try to hide them. There were times along my grief journey when I felt jealous—but I know now that was a normal part of this process.

Christmas happened about two months after Blaine's passing. I did not get as many cards as I had in other years. I am sure people wondered, *Should I send Angela a card so soon after Blaine's passing?* Many would not have known my address because I had moved, or maybe they did not send cards that year. Yet, when I did get a card in the mail, it did not make me happy either. It reminded me of the joyful family pictures I could no longer have with Blaine. I regretted that we did not take more pictures. I envied those with perfect family picture Christmas cards.

I was also jealous of people who had husbands to complain about. We have all done it, I am sure, complaining about things our husbands did, like dumping his coat on the floor or making a mess. But losing a loved one makes you hypersensitive to things people say. In those moments, I wished I had a husband to complain about.

People are going to work. They are going to town. They are shopping and carrying on with business. Your world has come to a grinding halt, and everyone else on TV, social media, and all around the world is carrying on like nothing happened. Initially, I received a lot of messages and calls from people, which was helpful. Understandably, people got busier and focused on their priorities. Then I did not hear from them as much. There is an expectation that you will feel better and get on with your life. But that takes more time than most people expect.

I was jealous of everyone who was living their life without grief. When I went out for a walk in the park, for example, if I saw a couple holding hands, a family sitting together, or friends driving by in a car together, I would get jealous. *It's unfair. They have their spouses and their fun, and I don't.* Then I would think, *I am jealous, and it's wrong.* So now, on top of feeling sad about being alone, I was feeling guilt, shame, and jealousy. At first, I did my best to stuff it down. That did not work.

Brené Brown says this about shame:

If you put shame in a petri dish, it needs three ingredients to grow exponentially: secrecy, silence, and judgment. If you put the same amount of shame in the petri dish and douse it with empathy, it can't survive.

When I could tell my coach or friends and family about my jealousy, they acknowledged my pain and offered me empathy. Over time, I learned to have compassion for myself. That meant giving myself the permission to feel jealous. After all, none of this was easy. Finally, when I accepted it was okay and expressed my pain, I started to release it. Now I can look at a couple and remember how in love Blaine and I were. I remember how good it felt to walk with him and talk to him about anything. These memories make me happy, fill me with love, and open my heart. Now, when I see couples in the park, I see them as a gift. They are a gentle reminder of how beautiful love truly is.

Anger

In those nine months that Blaine was sick, like I said, I was angry at God. I was also angry at the universe and anyone else "up there" for not helping us when we needed it most. *Where were those angels everyone was talking about? We prayed, meditated, and did all the right things. Why did it seem like nothing we did helped? Why was Blaine's sickness necessary? Why was this happening to us? What did we do to deserve it?* I think it scared Blaine to see me angry. It scared me too. So, at one point, I made a vow not to be angry anymore.

Suppressing anger can contribute to various mental and physical health issues, so it is important to express it. Yet, in our culture, anger is not a welcome emotion. Expression of emotions like anger can be associated with being weak or unstable. *How can I express my hidden anger when I believe it is not allowed?* It felt unsafe for me to even think about my anger. I asked myself, *If I were angry about something, what would it be?* Making a list of potential anger triggers felt less threatening than experiencing anger. My list was longer than I thought it would be. I gave myself permission to feel the anger that I "might" feel.

If you think you might be suppressing your anger, I recommend you try making a list for yourself. Here are a few things that came up for me. I was angry that:

- my husband died from colon cancer. I resented that had we caught it sooner, he might still be alive.
- my daughter lost her dad and went through a terrible cancer scare with her own husband at the same time.
- my grandchildren would not know their grandpa.
- I could not experience retirement fun with Blaine. Blaine never got his trip across Canada in the motorhome, and he never got that Mustang.
- Blaine left me alone and burdened me with more responsibilities.
- the medical system was unable to heal Blaine.
- everyone is aware of cancer yet powerless to take action.

There were so many more things on the list! It is gut wrenching and painful working through these powerful emotions, but I knew I had to do the work. I had to express the anger and move the energy, or I would carry that burden. It is like carrying a sack of potatoes around everywhere you go. You have to expend so much energy hanging onto something you no longer need. As I explain in future chapters, the anger I was suppressing was appearing as symptoms in my physical body. We cannot sit idly by and hope time will heal our wounds. We have to work through them.

It is possible to express anger in a healthy way. If you are having trouble, get someone to help guide you through it. It takes time, patience, and understanding. You might scream, yell, beat pillows, or throw clothes all over your room! Find something safe you can do. There was an episode of the TV show *Gray's Anatomy*[7] in which the doctors all danced out their emotions. Perhaps a good exercise workout will be the ticket. Whatever you can do to move the energy up and out of your body will lighten your emotional body and keep physical symptoms from appearing in the future.

Fear

Grief can amplify and intensify fear for several reasons. Losing a loved one leaves us uncertain, vulnerable, and apprehensive about moving forward. Our mind has trouble making sense of all the changes, which creates a complex emotional response. Our future as we imagined it is gone. We do not know who or what we can trust, and this disrupts our sense of security, stability, and predictability. Friends and family may not know how to support us. We feel alone. It shakes us to the core.

There are so many situations in which you may experience fear. You may be afraid of having an emotional breakdown in front of your colleagues at work or your children at home. Maybe you worry about stopping emotion once it starts. You might be afraid of being alone in your home. It is normal to feel afraid of losing someone or something else. Perhaps you fear not grieving properly or never experiencing happiness again. Your loss can have you questioning your existence and your faith. You may even fear your own mortality.

It is common for fear to be associated with thoughts and concerns about the future. Our mind is trying to keep us safe, looking ahead, trying to come up with future scenarios that might be dangerous and warn us about them. Your mind finds comfort in routine and predictability. It knows that what you did in the past kept you alive. It needs predictability to feel safe. Yet you cannot go back to the way things were.

There is a popular phrase that fear is "False Expectations Appearing Real." Often, fear arises from expectations developed in the mind rather than an actual danger or threat. It is important to distinguish what is a threat and what the mind is creating as a potential threat.

It is said we cannot be in a state of fear if we are in a state of love. They are opposing forces. Choosing thought forms related to love—such as compassion, understanding, and acceptance—helps to lessen fear. These energies are expansive and bring about feelings of peace.

Just as we assure a child who has woken up in the night with a nightmare, we can reassure ourselves that at this moment we are okay. This is a form of self-love. We can find things that bring us comfort in these situations and allow ourselves to breathe. Then we can check what thoughts and beliefs are creating fear and reframe them.

The following is an account of one of my experiences with fear.

A few months after Blaine's passing, I was having digestive issues, and my doctor felt it was best to do a colonoscopy and a scope. This procedure can cause fear and anxiety. I had undergone this process before, and it had been unsuccessful. The surgeon told me, "You have a very twisty bowel." Now, eight years later, this new surgeon assured me that the technology today is more advanced. "Try again," he said. I was not convinced. I had developed a mistrust of the medical system. It went as far back as when my son was little, perhaps farther, and my experience with Blaine had added more fear. It was difficult. My memories were fresh and unpleasant. So, when the hospital called with the date for my procedure, intense fear rose inside me.

Since the issues I had been having had all but disappeared, this would be more of a checkup for me. I did not expect to die from a colonoscopy, so there was not much to be concerned about. Still, I was worried. I had to surrender to the fact that this procedure was for my highest and best.

Cathleena told me, "The more you can be in the present moment as you are going about your day, the better. The more you can breathe and allow what you feel, the more comfortable this will feel." I had to be gentle with myself. I learned it is all practice. When you push fear away, it pushes back.

My fear continued to return again and again. Cathleena suggested I sit with it. It was terribly uncomfortable, and hard not to resist it. There was so much tension in my chest, I could barely stand it. I tried to release the tension with my breath, and it helped some, but when I least expected it, it came roaring back. It kept reminding me what had happened before, what had happened to Blaine, and the stories I had heard about others who had experienced a colonoscopy. Most of their stories had happy endings. Yet, that did not seem to matter to my mind. If there is a risk, your mind is going to let you know—and my mind did just that.

As the day approached, my fear intensified. I tried telling others about it, breathing, and distracting myself. I also practiced putting myself in the present moment. All these things provided temporary relief, and the fear came back. I knew once the procedure was over, I would feel better, but I wanted to go in feeling calm, and I was determined to release my fear. We cannot make fear go away or fix it. We have to embrace it.

I judged myself: *Compared to what Blaine went through and what others have gone through*, I thought, *this is a small thing. I am making more of this than I need to.* That thinking was not helping. In fact, it made things worse. I did not know what else to do, so I asked my higher self for help. I knew it is important to give your guides permission to help, so I did that too. As I sat in the quiet, I remembered being at Blaine's bedside after the doctors had done his colonoscopy and scope. The surgeon said, "We didn't catch it in time. It is stage 4. You can usually get up to five years with proper treatment."

Blaine, who was groggy at the time, said, "Did you say you caught it in time?"

The doctor said, "No, we did not."

The memory was so real, I felt like I had been punched in the gut (as Blaine had always described it), reliving that moment in real time. As the emotion came up, I tapped all my EFT points. I cried and released my emotion. Then I remembered when Blaine and I left the hospital. I was breaking down. He was trying to console me. I felt so weak. Try as I might, I could not be the strong one.

Once that memory faded, another memory came up: dropping Blaine off for the chemotherapy treatment a few days before he died. I felt such hesitation and trepidation—I could not imagine his body taking one more round of this. I barely recognized him anymore because the treatment and the disease had taken their toll on him.

The emotions rose in me again, and I allowed them to come. When I could finally see through my tears, I found my Chromebook. Sitting with the emotion, I poured my feelings out on the page, and I felt something shift. But somehow I knew it was not over.

My higher self had more to show me. Recently, a client had signed up for a complimentary one-on-one session with me for her grief. She had lost her husband and was angry at the staff at the medical facility. She felt their mistreatment had killed him. Understandably, her feelings were intense. I believe there is a reason for people entering your life. *What had brought her to me?* I realized she was mirroring the anger within me. When we lose someone, it can bring up emotion from the past. I realized I had not processed everything that had happened with Curtise or other incidents from my past. A part of me felt the medical system had failed us. As I sat in my sadness and anger, I reflected on letting Blaine go with the nurse for that last chemotherapy treatment. That nurse had to make a decision every day. She had to go into that hospital, up to that chemotherapy ward, and give of herself in a way that I will never fully understand. At that moment, I felt a rush of deep sadness. I felt profound gratitude for that beautiful nurse and all the medical staff. There is something so horrible and yet so beautiful about what they do. After sitting with my thoughts for a while, it came to me that I wanted to leave a small gesture of gratitude for the cancer nurses who were so helpful to Blaine. Somehow, my feelings had shifted from fear to gratitude and love. When you are in love, fear becomes quiet.

This brought significant relief. I felt lighter. I felt tender and vulnerable. I embraced the quiet. Before the evening ended, another memory came to me. I was leaving Blaine's hospital room after spending the day with him, the day after his first treatment. He had been vomiting for two days. The seventy-five-mile drive to the hospital, combined with the chemotherapy, had resulted in Blaine experiencing uncontrollable nausea. I barely made it out the door of Blaine's room before tears started rolling down my face. I passed Blaine's doctor in the hallway. I was so embarrassed. I felt I needed to stay strong, and I did it to the best of my ability.

After all these memories came forward, I saw myself as I was back then—disheartened, alone, and afraid. I had no idea at the time it could get that bad. Watching Blaine's suffering was unbearable—and I did not know then that it was only the beginning. As I sat reminiscing, I realized I was holding on to all that emotion. Suddenly, it made sense: *What I had pushed down in those moments has to come up for release.* Releasing those emotions made room for me to choose gratitude and compassion for myself, Blaine, and the entire medical staff. I thought about that doctor and how he did everything he could to advocate for Blaine. I recalled overhearing him on the phone pleading with the Cancer Center. He had wanted a particular anti-nausea medication that could help Blaine with his symptoms. Of course it was more expensive. Because of this, the Cancer Center would not go for it. I thought about all I was going through in that space. I felt deep compassion for anyone, including myself, facing the horrifying experience of watching a loved one suffer. I was so disappointed and helpless, yet there was a feeling of gratitude and love for the doctor and the medical staff for their incredible service.

Healer and spiritual coach Suzanne Alexandria gifted me a healing session, and on the day before my test, Suzanne guided me through witnessing and feeling more of the fear. In that session, I realized direct communication with our bodies can be powerful. I had never thought about talking to my body. I decided I would reassure my body through touch, voice, and intention. I told my body, *We will get through this.*

I woke up the next morning with a sinking feeling, like something terribly wrong was going to happen. After I acknowledged my fear, I tried to reframe my thoughts. *After what happened to Blaine, it is easy to justify a colonoscopy as an important prevention tool. I should be grateful there is a test. I could see this as an opportunity to face my fear. It may bring healing and growth. Perhaps I can let go of my mistrust on some level.* I had an hour-and-a-half drive to get to the hospital. The fear was still there. Strangely, though, I was able to keep myself in the present. I was tapping, breathing, and listening to music along the way. When I got to the hospital, I felt extra nervous. I asked my guides and angels to help me, and I gave them permission to help in any way that would serve my highest good. I thought about the caring nurses and doctors in that hospital and trusted they would do their best to look after me. I told my body: *I've got your back no matter what happens, and we are going to be okay. My higher self and I, we have got this!*

Things went better than I had anticipated. Upon reaching the waiting area, there were few people. The nurses took me in immediately, which surprised me. They were in a rush to get me through so the surgeon could get to the OR. Things went quickly. Even though it felt like my heart was beating out of my chest with fear, the staff helped me feel safe and comfortable. I felt some intense pain off and on through the procedure, but with the help of the medical team and some wonderful drugs, we made it through.

Before I left, I delivered a special gift to the nurses at the Cancer Center. I wrote them a long note in a card about how I recognized the amazing service they provide. In that note, I expressed how grateful I was and included a gift card for Tim Horton's. They were not there to receive it, so I set it on the desk. It felt good to bring a sweetness to what was such a horrific memory for me.

We have all experienced some type of fear. Some of us have a fear of spiders, or heights, or snakes. These fears may seem extreme and unjustified to those who do not understand. I think life challenges us with these things to help us learn and grow. My colonoscopy challenge had not been one of life or death. Walking Blaine through his journey with colon cancer was, and that experience directly affected my level of fear in this circumstance.

There were other techniques I used to help me work through my fear. I used drumming, sounding, and tapping to release energy.

- With drumming, any drum will work and you can make whatever sound you feel like making. You cannot do it wrong!

- Sounding is the same. Sounding is an energy healing technique that involves using vocal sounds, such as chanting, toning, or singing, to promote healing and balance in the body and mind. Sound vibrations can have a profound impact on our energy and can help to release blockages and restore harmony. You do not have to be musical to do these sounding exercises. In fact, it might be better if you are not. I grew up with music, playing instruments such as the organ, flute, and piano in addition to singing and playing at musical festival competitions at the provincial level. I also played flute in a school band, and, later in life, picked up the guitar. When I was teaching, I delighted in being able to offer music to students and have fond memories of school musicals such as *Grease*, *Footloose*, *The Lion King*, and *The Grinch*. I enjoyed music, and it got me through some tough times growing up. The difference I found with sounding is you do not have to worry about whether you are in tune or whether it sounds good. You just make sounds! It is quite freeing to do once you allow yourself the opportunity.

- Tapping is also helpful for releasing fear. I tapped along with EFT practitioners on YouTube. A quick search on "Tapping for Fear" will provide you with many from which to choose.

Anything you can do to release your fear will be helpful. Sometimes it can be frustrating because it can feel like nothing is working. Each time we show up for ourselves and try a technique, we are investing in a better outcome for the future. We are learning and practicing what works for us. It takes persistence, patience, and practice.

Guilt and Shame

There is a difference between shame and guilt. Guilt is saying, "I did something bad." Shame is saying, "I am bad." The difference is that we can separate what we did from who we are, and guilt does not define us. Often, we can recognize guilt when we use the words "could have" or "should have." If we are saying or hearing those words, they can point to an underlying feeling of guilt. Guilt can be useful if we use it to correct a behavior and we can make amends. It is when we cannot fix a mistake that guilt can persist. For example, as long as I felt I could have done something more to save Blaine, my guilt endured.

If we allow guilt to fester, it can persist and become shame. My thoughts could have become: "I was a poor caregiver. I am not enough." Brené Brown defines shame as "the intensely painful belief that we are flawed and, therefore, unworthy of love and belonging."[8] Deep down, we feel there is something we have done or failed to do that has brought us to this place of worthlessness. In this state, we experience extreme lows. We may not imagine how we will ever rise above them.

In order to overcome feelings of shame, we want to disconnect our identity from the emotion in the statements we make: *I am not a bad person. Rather, I had an awful experience.* The more we talk to others about our guilt, the better and healthier we become. It keeps us from moving into shame, and it can help others by giving them the safe space to share their own feelings of guilt.

At some point, many people who have lost a loved one feel guilty for being happy. Survival guilt is when you get through something when others do not. Some might feel responsible for the outcome. For example, I felt for a long while that had we done things differently, we might have prevented Blaine's suffering. Maybe we could have had more time. Maybe we could have saved him. If we let it, this guilty self-talk can become overwhelming. Just because a person feels guilty does not mean they are guilty. If we could predict the future, often, we would make different decisions. If you look at the definition of guilt, it involves having committed an actual offense. Ask yourself, "Did I mean to cause harm?" We are all doing the best we can to make a decision in the time and space we are in, and with the knowledge we have. I had to accept that I could not save Blaine. I could not have prevented his cancer or his death.

When we are experiencing shame or guilt, our mind is making up a story that does not align with our fundamental truth or our core beliefs, and there is emotional and physical discomfort in our bodies. Our physical discomfort is a clue that a false belief is governing us. We can look at the stories we are telling ourselves and ask ourselves: "Is this story true?" Eventually, we can reframe our stories in a loving, compassionate way.

If we just grow guilt, guilt blocks growth! Sometimes, the only way you can feel better about the past is to edit the present. In my case, I have thought about what my priorities were when I did not make time for my family. I know what would have been lost for my students if I had not done things the way I did. I must accept that my time was not wasted. I was doing what felt right in my heart at the time. I have learned that in the future, I can make time for others in honor of Blaine.

Can you accept that something that happened in your life may have happened because life is unpredictable, chaotic, and, in so many ways, incomprehensible? Sometimes it is easier to blame ourselves or someone else for what happens than to think that some things are out of our control. To get past the guilt and shame, it is important to acknowledge all our feelings and emotions as they arise— even the uncomfortable ones. We cannot be in a hurry to bypass these or make up positive statements to get past them. We must recognize them. If you cannot deal with the pain at this moment, that is okay. Take it in small steps. Our body knows what we need to heal, and, inevitably, we will get another chance to sit with those emotions when the time is right for us. Do not worry if these thoughts and feelings come around again and again. It is how the process works. We do not have to worry that we are moving backward on our journey. We are healing more deeply. There will be highs and lows. Within that turmoil, our job is to come back to a sense of calm. Sometimes we can feel peaceful, knowing this, too, shall pass.

You are here to follow your joy and share it with others. Nothing you have done or said can change that. Focusing on your future and how you will spread your love and kindness meaningfully is going to fulfill your life from now on. We will never feel true happiness if we are beating ourselves up continually over the same story day after day. Instead, we will end up anxious, depressed, and miserable. Watch your inner dialogue for times you are experiencing guilt and/or shame. Show yourself love and compassion for the difficult things you are going through. You deserve to be happy and fulfilled.

Exercises:

- Often, we have a good reason to be angry after a loss. Think about your loss and your life situation right now. If you were angry about something, what could it be? Read your list out loud. What are some ways you might be able to release the anger inside of you?
- Use the exercise above to explore the emotions of jealousy, fear, guilt, and shame. Talk about these with a coach or write them in your journal. Express yourself through art, music, or in other creative ways.
- Practice Mark Waldman's sixty-second exercises to reduce stress and anxiety.[9]

Chapter 6

———

Our Body and Emotion

Physical Symptoms Related to Grief

Right after Christmas, I flew to Vancouver Island to spend a few weeks with my parents. I needed time to just be and figure things out. It had only been two months since Blaine's death. I had spent Christmas with Blaine's family and was thinking into the new year, planning. *What will I do with myself?* Around this time, I started having stomach issues. I could not eat much. Since I was staying with my parents at the time, I ended up in the emergency room on Vancouver Island in so much pain. I thought it was an ulcer. They sent me away saying they could find nothing wrong. This was the beginning of the physical symptoms related to my grief.

There is a connection between our mind, body, and spirit. Powerful emotions, such as those brought on by grief, can manifest physically. I used to think my body had its own governance. It did what it did when it did it. Of course, I knew that exercising the body, eating properly, and getting good rest was important, and I knew stress was not a good thing. But I never realized how valuable it is to pay attention to and communicate with my body. Even more amazing was my discovery that my body communicates with me!

Authors like the late motivational speaker Louise Hay and trainer Wendi Jensen have written books about illness and discomfort in the body and how each of our body parts has a corresponding emotional connection. For example, they say grief is associated with the lungs. Many people describe grief as the inability to breathe. There were several moments after Blaine's passing when I felt a tight feeling in my chest. Mom did a tapping session with me to release the emotion. Within a few minutes, I could feel the pressure in my chest release and then I could take a full breath. I was holding the energy of grief in my lungs and as soon as I was willing to let it go, I felt better. (I have included the tapping script to help with this at the end of this chapter.)

As I noted earlier, emotions are "energy in motion." If we hold on to emotion, we are blocking the energy flow. Over time, that will cause discomfort in our physical body.

When I returned from my trip to Mom and Dad's, my stomach issues continued. I saw my doctor. She treated me with antacids, and they helped some, so she felt I had a bit of inflammation. In February, I still felt called to go to Sedona to experience the energy vortices and the big red rocks in the hills, so I traveled to Mesa, Arizona, to see my Sharon and Don. Sharon and Don said they would drive me to Sedona, as it was a nice drive from Mesa.

As part of the trip, I booked a week-long retreat with Spirit Quest Retreats. Sharon and Don dropped me off near the Sedona Airport. I rented a car for a week and stayed at the Sky Ranch Lodge, a beautiful hotel set in the quiet serenity of the desert, a short walk from the airport. At the Spirit Quest Center I did several healing sessions a day for five days. The sessions included working with a shaman, working with a practitioner on childhood trauma, and doing breathwork, massage, sound healing, chakra balancing, and more.

From my hotel, I had easy access to the Airport Mesa hiking trail. One day, I decided to walk this trail on my own. One of the most well-known vortices in Sedona is called the Airport Vortex (because of its proximity to the airport). It is known for its masculine energy, which is said to promote clarity, focus, and spiritual awakening. I had never walked a trail like this before. The views are panoramic. I ventured out on the path around 8:00 a.m.

As I walked along the red-earth path, I was overcome by fear several times. *What if I don't get back? What if a wild animal comes out of the rocks? I shouldn't be doing this. I know nothing about hiking. No one will ever find me out here!* I looked over the mesa at the hills. The view was amazing, and my legs trembled as I stared out over the edge. *It is a long way down there if I ever slip and lose my footing.* I needed to be back at the hotel for an inner-child healing session by 10:45 a.m. I had read somewhere that the hike would take about 1.5 hours. I hoped what I had googled was correct. I kept walking. The bushes, red rocks, prickly pear cacti, and twisted junipers kept urging me on even though a big part of me wanted to turn back. I forged on, believing it should loop around. After all, they call it the "Airport Loop."

At one point, when the trail started to climb up toward the airport, I realized I was committed. I had come this far. I kept going around the back side of the mesa. I came to a fork in the path. I chose the fork to the right. Again, I felt fear. *What if I can't get back? What if I miss my session?* I thought about my life and how I had organized and planned it all out before I lost Blaine. I was not someone who took risks like this. *Can I just trust and know the trail will lead me back?* I need not have worried because later I noticed where the two trails, the left fork and the right fork, met. I kept going until I recognized my hotel. I was relieved—until I realized I was on the wrong side of the airport road. The airport road ends at the top of the mesa, and I had ended up on the embankment on the opposite side of the road from my hotel. Again, I felt the fear. *I am going the wrong way! I've never been good at directions. Blaine was good at directions. I am lost!* I found a place where I could cross the road and a trail that seemed to be going the right direction. I noticed the ground was the same red color as the path I had started out on, so I kept following it. Hoping I was not going to overshoot the parking lot and arrive in town somewhere, I kept walking. Finally, I recognized the parking lot. Relieved, I got into my rental car and headed back to the hotel. Never would I have guessed this would be the beginning of a journey to healing my fear of walking life's journey alone. I could never have known that what was to come in the next few days in Sedona would change the trajectory of my life. I made it to the inner-child healing session on time, and it was there that I wrote this account of my journey. It was also then and there that I decided I would someday write a book.

The trip to Sedona was transformational. I had never stayed on my own in a place I had never been. I had never rented a car and driven in a strange place on my own. I left the retreat feeling like my life had taken on a whole new path. I was looking ahead with more confidence. I fell in love with Sedona.

Before I left Arizona, the stomach issues rose up again. I got through them, and when I got home, the doctors did X-rays, ordered an ultrasound, and did additional bloodwork. I made an appointment with my naturopath, Leshia. As the days went by, I got so exhausted, I could not even walk twenty minutes without feeling like I might collapse. I tried to pack my suitcase to go on a Donna Eden European River Cruise with Mom in March. I was thinking, *I will never make it.*

Luckily, I thought to send Leshia my blood tests the weekend before we had to leave. She noticed my liver numbers showed stress and concluded that my gall bladder may very well be the issue. We decided I should take the trip anyway, and she gave me a strict diet plan to follow to help the liver. It took time, but several days after I changed my diet, I regained my strength and enjoyed the trip. Mom and I were on a boat with Donna Eden and a group of energy healers, so that, coupled with the new diet and time away, was just what I needed.

A while after I returned from my trip, I got the ultrasound done. Gallstones. As I look back, it was fortunate I had reached out for help in a variety of ways. Sometimes it takes more than one practitioner to get to the bottom of an issue. Energetically speaking, stomach issues can be related to worry and overthinking. The gallbladder and liver are associated with anger (and I later discovered I was suppressing these emotions). Knowing these connections can give us clues to where our energy is blocked and what emotional healing we need to do to get it flowing again.

Just like we can get these signs and messages from our bodies as a way of communication, we can communicate directly with our bodies. When we have parts that are sore, for example, we can direct our focus to those areas to help the healing process. I mention Donna Eden because her teachings are profound. You do not have to be a trained practitioner to incorporate many of the exercises into your daily routine. So much of her material is free on YouTube. Donna speaks about how your hands can help move the energy in your body. We can place our hands over the part of our body that is feeling the pain and focus on healing energy there. We can weave figure eights over the affected area. We can comfort and reassure those parts by talking to them and letting them know, "I am listening."

Reiki works in a similar way. We can place our hands over different areas of our bodies to remove energy blocks and help our energy flow. By getting quiet in meditation and raising our vibration, we can send healing energy to all our cells. Doing energy work is building a relationship with our body just as we would build a relationship with our spirit, God, or the Universe. It is also important that we see ourselves as a whole and not simply a body if we want to continue to be healthy physically and emotionally.

Faith, Trust, and Surrender

About five months following Blaine's passing, unique challenges presented themselves. It seemed unfair and untimely. We cannot always understand these things with our human minds, and I have learned to not try to figure it all out. Our minds are like computers trying to process a large file—they spin and spin. Sometimes awful things happen, and it feels like we are victims of some powerful force working against us. We wonder, *What did I do to deserve this?* I believe the universe works for us, not against us, even though sometimes it sure does not feel like it!

I had just gotten back from my river cruise trip in Europe. The day I came home, I tested positive for COVID-19. I had been gone three weeks. Now I would be home alone for another ten days. A big snowstorm snapped off hundreds of power poles in our area, and we were without power for five days in a Saskatchewan winter! So, there I was in the dark; sick, cold, unable to go anywhere, and no one could come visit me. Then I discovered the floor in my entryway was sloshing wet underneath the laminate flooring and it had swelled. Oh, oh, major problem!

On Easter Monday, Curtise and Sheldon came over and helped me dig up the floor. We found a lot of water, but where was it coming from? I called a plumber, and the investigation began. The contractors had to rip up part of the concrete slab my house had been built on. I do not have a basement, and there is in-floor heat. One issue was that the line for the in-floor heat loop to the garage was leaking. That problem was solved by shutting off that loop. This meant I would have to put in heat for the garage. The second issue was harder to find. It involved a jack hammer and a cement saw—and no water service in the house for a couple of days. The contractors lifted enormous boulders of cement out of my house, leaving a gaping hole in the floor. They removed part of a wall. After the dust settled (literally), they discovered a major waterline was leaking. It was a big challenge, but it was a relief to find the root of the problem. Now we could fix it. I needed contractors to pour new cement, replace the flooring, and rebuild the wall. I got my insurance broker to suggest a plumber and someone to pour cement. My next-door neighbor suggested someone to put in the floor.

It was all too much. I was overwhelmed with emotion. At first, I thought it was silly to cry over something like a floor.

Really? It's just a floor. I sat looking at Blaine's picture and I sobbed. I thought, *If you were here, you would know what to do. You could help me through this. You would know who to call.* I let myself think, *My husband died, I got sick, the power went out, and now there is a gaping hole in the floor. Why can't things go right?* I had to let that out.

Once those negative streams of thoughts passed, I investigated my beliefs. *I've got good reasons to be upset. It isn't fair.* Deep down, I knew, *I am more capable than I give myself credit for, and it all will work out okay.* Someone pointed out to me our human tendency to think of the worst-case scenario and prepare for that. I was offered the idea that I could change my thinking to focus on the best-case scenario and plan for that. What a simple but valuable idea! So, I sat and thought about all the best-case scenarios I could for this water situation. Then I said a prayer, and I surrendered to one of those outcomes ... or something even better!

I read a book by Tom T. Moore called *The Gentle Way*. In it he explains the power of asking for a benevolent outcome for any situation. The book was hugely helpful. There were examples of how he had prayed to his angels and had amazing results. I prayed for a most benevolent outcome for the water leak issue. *Who knows what good could come of this? It might be something I could not have ever imagined.*

At around the same time, I discovered there were some shingles missing from my roof. I got the name of a roofer. When he came to look, he found the skylight in my bathroom was leaking and had damaged the roof. He fixed the roof, replaced the shingles, and boarded up the skylight. Not much later, I went outside to get something out of the detached garage in the back. The floor was wet, and the drywall was moldy. Upon investigation, I found that the garage was sitting directly on the cement. There was no stem wall in between the two-by-fours and the cement slab under the garage, and the two-by-fours were rotten. My place was bursting with leaks!

Someone pointed out to me that there may have been some energetic symbolism in all that was happening. Symbolically, water is associated with purification, healing, and transformation. It can represent the flow of emotions, the depths of the subconscious mind, and the power of intuition. It is also a symbol of rebirth and connecting with ourselves and others on a deep emotional level.

Through this chain of unfortunate events, I realized I am resilient. Once I let the emotions rise up and out, I made good decisions using my intuition and guidance from my higher self. I came to understand that just because Blaine was not with me physically, that did not mean he was not with me in spirit—so I connected with him to ask for help. I learned that I can call upon my higher guides as well as angels here on earth. I only need to reach out, have faith, and trust that things will work out.

The plumbers, carpenter, and roofer were all great. When it came to the garage, Calvin came to the rescue. Everyone was cheerful and happy and made a precarious situation (somewhat) more of an adventure than a catastrophe. Today, I have running water, a solid floor, a leak-free roof, and a solid garage—and I am so grateful for all of it.

Sometimes things go terribly wrong, and when that happens, it is okay to be upset. It is okay to throw your hands up in the air and ask, "Why?!" It is normal to have emotion around it all. You can do this for as long as you need to. No matter how bad it gets, remember, you have a team guiding you and protecting you through it all. You can put your faith and trust in your higher self. Do what you can. Ask for help with the rest. Continue on with your life in the most joyful way possible.

References:

1. Donna Eden: Figure 8 Exercise, demonstrated by Dondi Dahlin.[10]
2. Check out the list of Louise Hay's list of common ailments and corresponding emotional roots.[11]
3. Sign up to Louise Hay's website to receive free affirmations to heal your body. Her website offers many meditations to calm and heal the body as well.[12]
4. Reading Suggestion: *You Can Heal Your Life* by Louise Hay.

Tapping Exercise:

If you have never tapped before, I recommend you do some guided tapping just so you have the idea of the process. Search "tapping" on YouTube. A good one to try is called "How to Tap with Jessica Ortner." It is so easy to do. The tapping script below was created by my mother, Elaine Winquist, a certified EFT practitioner, and me.

- Side of Hand: Even though I feel like I am unable to breathe, I am honoring and accepting myself and all these feelings. (Keep tapping and repeat three times.)
- (EB) Eyebrow: I feel like I cannot breathe.
- (SE) Side of Eye: This is frightening.
- (UE) Under Eye: This deep pain.
- (UN) Under Nose: This grief.
- (CH) Chin: So much sadness.
- (CB) Collarbone: This heaviness in my chest.
- (UA) Under Arm: I take in a breath now.
- (TH) Top of Head: I am choosing to release some of these feelings as I release my breath.
- EB: (keep tapping while you take a breath in)
- SE: (keep tapping as you breathe out) I am releasing this fear.
- UE: (keep tapping as you breathe in)

- UN: (breathe out while saying) I am releasing this heaviness.
- CH: (keep tapping as you breathe in)
- CB: (breathe out while saying) I give myself permission to release some of this grief.
- UA: (keep tapping while you breathe in)
- TH: It is okay not to be okay right now. I remember to be kind to myself.
- Side of Hand: Even though this grief takes my breath away as I process this loss, I am choosing to honor and accept myself and all these feelings. (Repeat three times.)
- EB: I am choosing to relax as I remember it is okay to not be okay.
- SE: It is not a wonder I can hardly breathe.
- UE: So much to do and think about.
- UN: It is okay not to be okay in this moment.
- CH: I can be very kind to myself as I take a breath in.
- CB: I am open to releasing some of this pain as I breathe out.
- UA: I take a breath in.
- TH: I release these feeling of grief as I breathe out.
- EB: I am remembering it is okay if I do not feel okay right now.
- SE: I am doing the best I can, and I honor myself for that.
- UE: I am open to accepting help when I need it.
- UN: I am practicing asking for help when I need to.
- CH: I am doing the best I can, and that is perfectly okay.
- CB: Sometimes just breathing may be all I can manage.
- UA: I am okay.
- TH: All of these feelings.
- EB: I am not sure how I can cope.
- SE: I am not sure how I can even process all these feelings.

- UE: I am remembering to be very kind to myself.
- UN: I remember to give myself grace.
- CH: To accept help when it is offered.
- CB: I give myself permission to ask for help when I need it.
- UA: It is okay to not be okay right now. I just need to breathe and do the best I can while I process all these feelings.
- Side of Hand: Even though I can hardly breathe, I am remembering to be very kind to myself as I honor and accept myself and all these feelings. (Repeat three times.)
- TH: I am remembering it is okay to just breathe.
- EB: I remember it is okay to cry or not to cry.
- SE: I am learning how to look after myself.
- UE: I am learning to release some of this pain.
- UN: It is okay to let go as I am able; there is no timeline.
- CH: I am releasing these feelings to make room for healing.
- CB: As I breathe in and out, I think of ways to honor my loved one.
- UA: I can do that best by taking care of myself.
- Side of the hand: It is safe for me to breathe as I learn to honor myself.

Take a deep breath and check in with your body. You can repeat this tap several times, checking in each time. If particular phrases are especially helpful, repeat them several times. Notice how this simple technique can help you calm and center yourself again. You are doing the work of releasing the emotion through this practice. You are working toward healing your pain.

Aerial view of Clement Ranch captured by Curtise using a drone.

The iconic red barn featuring the Clement Ranch brand —C—, originally Clayton's (Blaine's father) brand. Blaine can be seen in the foreground carrying a bucket, likely returning from feeding a calf.

Blaine armed with a Super Soaker, ready for a water fight
with nieces and nephews at Cypress Hills Park.

Blaine and Angela Clement.

Curtise and Blaine enjoying a Saskatchewan
Roughriders football game in Regina.

Whitney and Blaine celebrating at Whitney's graduation ceremony.

The Clement family at Curtise and Jennifer's wedding (July 11, 2020).
From left to right: Whitney, Curtise, Angela, and Blaine.

Family portrait at Sheldon and Whitney's wedding (July 23, 2022).
From left to right: Angela, Whitney, Sheldon, Jennifer, and Curtise.

PART III

Acknowledging the Loss

Chapter 7

Letting Go

Grief comes in many forms—and it is not just related to death and dying. Life is continually changing, and as it changes, we learn to accept that what is in the past is lost. Each time we experience loss, grief is there to help us through. For example, we do not think of the sadness a young mother feels when her little one starts school as grief. But it is. That empty-nest feeling when your baby goes off to college or university? Also grief. When you move to a new home, you grieve for your old home and your friends. When you retire, it is the same. We let go of the old to let in the new. When you let go, it is normal to grieve. Letting go helps you move forward.

When we have been thinking about retirement or our babies leaving the nest, we have readied ourselves. We know it is coming. We have been thinking about it, preparing for it. It is difficult to let go. There is change. This change is not the same as losing a loved one, of course.

I was not prepared or ready to let go of Blaine so soon. We had our whole retirement ahead of us—until we did not. Letting go is difficult. The physical form as we knew it is gone. Our loved one is no longer here, and it feels like a part of us went with them. This is what Eckhart Tolle refers to as attachment to our ego, that part of ourselves we associate with our identity. For example, I was Blaine's wife. *Who am I now if I am not Blaine's wife?* We had our friends, our life, our dreams. When Blaine left, I wanted to go back to the way things were. Knowing I could not go back was painful. I resisted living a different life. My resistance brought me pain and suffering. I grieved not only for what I missed from the past but also for the future.

In our greatest suffering, we are forced to surrender to what is. As the Sufi proverb says, "When the ego weeps for what it has lost, the spirit rejoices for what it has found."[13] When someone you have loved is suddenly ripped from you, you are forced to realize they were a big part of your life, and that you no longer feel whole. Yet spiritually, you are whole. The spirit is the true essence of who you are. No matter what has happened to me in this life—even the loss of my most intimate relationship—my spirit, my essence, remains the same. It is not broken. It cannot be touched because it is infinite. Blaine's essence, too, is infinite. Our connection will be forever. It can never, ever change. This realization was the beginning of my awakening.

Letting go is the purpose for the grieving process. It is not easy. We cannot do it all at once. As I mourn, I let a little go at a time. When some event or topic of discussion activates my emotions, I do what I can, when I can, to let those painful emotions run through me. I do my best not to resist them. Instead I surrender and get curious: *What are they showing me?* I can start a journal and let them go by writing. I can take a walk, cry, or listen to music. There are many ways to let go. After I do that, I imagine what I want my future to look like. I start to build something new.

Over time, I look fondly at the past, grateful for the memories. I build meaning. This is the process of grief. It allows us to move forward. Even though it is difficult, it is the way to a fulfilling life.

Blaine and I share over thirty-five years of memories. The bond we have is strong and still exists. I am learning to connect with him differently. I am letting go of what I cannot change. Sometimes I resist. It hurts. It is okay. I am patient with myself. I know that when I let these things go, I am making room to do something that excites me, that gives me the space to discover who I am and what I want to be in this world. It makes room for passion and joy. I know Blaine is right here with me, helping me let go. I know he is delighted to be a part of my new journey, whatever that might be.

Attachment and Ego

In his book *The Power of Now*, Eckhart Tolle talks about "the pain body." All the pain we have felt sits within the energy field of our body. There might be anger, sadness, fear, or resentment sitting there waiting for some event to activate the emotion. When something activates the emotion, it influences our thoughts and behaviors. Eckhart talks about the pain body thriving on drama, conflict, and suffering. When Blaine passed, I could not stand watching a violent movie or the news. Not that I did not care what was happening in the world; I just realized I was much more sensitive. The news had the potential to activate my pain body and initiate suffering for me.

It was hard to retire, move, and lose my husband in the span of ten months. Yet, in a way, retirement was a gift because I could prioritize my time without distraction. I had to be aware of my sensitivity to conflict after my loss. While many of the experiences of being a school principal were exciting and fun, a conflict with a parent, a student, or a staff member from time to time was inevitable. Back then, I did not understand how that conflict was affecting me or how to navigate it. Now I could more easily create an environment where I would not be exposed to drama or discord that was not my own. Of course, sometimes events would happen that were not in my control. I realized that I had generated the conflict around me by focusing on it and reacting to it in a negative way. By listening to Eckhart Tolle and reading his books, I became aware of my pain body. I paid attention to it and observed it in action. I recognized what was happening energetically and realized, *I can let any drama around any situation go just by releasing that energetic frequency.*

At first, when I thought about the past and Blaine, I was overwhelmed with a sense of emptiness. I stuffed that feeling into my pain body. Then when something came along and activated my pain body, I reacted. For instance, once I was standing outside a restaurant waiting for a Chinese food order, enjoying the view. A silver Ford F-350 pulled up and parked. Instantly, I was reminded that Blaine had bought that kind of truck when he had retired, and he had very little time to enjoy it. My pain body responded. I was consumed by sadness. We call these grief bursts. The pain body influences our thoughts and behaviors, causing us to withdraw, cling to mementos, or react emotionally.

Eckhart Tolle encourages us to be with the pain, observe it, and allow it without judgment. The activation of the pain body is part of the grief process. I could embrace it, accept it, and have greater compassion for myself because of it. Once I was aware of what was happening, I could honor myself in my grief. Sharing my experience with empathic supporters helped. Now I can look at silver trucks without feeling charged with emotion. I have learned to embrace opportunities to heal my pain body, and this helps me find peace and acceptance while honoring memories.

Letting Go of Things

I was letting go of Blaine's things slowly. I had a bag in the closet, and I put things in it from time to time. Over the course of eight months, I let go of two or three bags full of clothes … mine and his. They were mostly things Blaine did not wear often, or things he wore when he got sick and lost all the weight. So, they did not have the meaning his older clothes had for me, and it seemed easier to let them go. Blaine's sister, Linda, took his jeans to make beautiful jean blankets—one for Curtise and Jen as a baby blanket after Benson was born, and one for Whitney and Sheldon as a wedding gift. I asked the kids if they wanted any of Blaine's clothes, and they took what they wanted.

For Christmas, I made little ornaments out of some articles of Blaine's clothing for each of his siblings and my family. My plan was to take some of his clothes, make some things, and then let the rest go. So, I thought I had it covered. The whole first year, it had been my challenge to meet all this grief head on. No matter how much it hurt, I would take a run at the wave and let it wash over me until it was gone and then enjoy the relief and the joy until the next wave. It was interesting how I chose to let go of his things slowly. I found it a tender and difficult process.

Letting go of Blaine's things seemed like the last big phase of letting go. His things connected me with memories. They seemed to hold his energy. As I held them close to me, I tried to remember or just get a sense of his presence. I put on the black leather gloves he wore when we went to town. There were sweatshirts that were his favorites. He wore these day after day, and they never seemed to wear out. He was a guy who often saved new things to wear for a special occasion. Some of them stayed in the closet for months, yet the raggy old sweaters he loved he wore again and again. They were the favorite sweaters he fed the cows in, and he wore the same ones to coach curling. Now they were extra special to me too. I held them up to my face, trying to get some kind of reminder of how things used to be from the scent. I tried to remember what it was like for us on the ranch. It brought tears to my eyes because no matter what it made me feel, he was not there.

I put the tree up again that year. I am fortunate to have a set of sand dollars painted by my grandmother that I hang on my tree every year, along with a couple of other meaningful ornaments. My good friend Sari had given me one ornament that said, "I have an angel in heaven. I call him my husband." Another one, a rocking chair, Curtise and Jen gave me. It had a little poem on it about saving a chair for our missing loved ones. The kids and I tried to make it out to Mom and Dad's for Christmas, but our flights got canceled at the last minute, and we ended up spending Christmas in a hotel in Calgary. We were there for five days. Then Sheldon and Whitney flew back to Saskatoon, and Curtise, Jen, Benson, and I, having a little more time, flew to Victoria and drove to Campbell River for a few days. It was disappointing for us and for Mom and Dad. They would have preferred to have us all there for Christmas. We made the best of it. Benson ended up getting sick, so we spent a quiet few days on the island.

When I got home, I wanted to make a few more ornaments for the nieces and nephews and some pillows from Blaine's shirts with team logos on them. It made sense that all his stuff could stay in the closet until I had finished. But I realized I had already taken out of the closet what I needed for that—and the inevitable showed itself. I had to reason with myself: *If I don't deal with Blaine's things now, when? And do I want to be uncomfortable until I do? This thing has been nagging at the back of my subconscious for nearly a year.*

Every time I went into my closet, I saw his things there. For me, as much as it was going to hurt, it was time. If you have never read Karen Kingston's *Clear Your Clutter with Feng Shui*, it is a great read, and I strongly advise it. Releasing things that no longer serve us can make room energetically for new things we want to bring in. Just like we can hold the energies of our emotions inside ourselves and stop the energetic flow in our bodies, we can stop the external flow by cluttering our spaces up with things that no longer bring us joy or serve us in some way. That lack of flow can have an effect on your health.

Having said all that, do not rush. Be gentle with yourself. Take your time. It can leave you tender. Take pictures of some of the things (or all of them), if that helps ease the attachment.

As I took Blaine's things out of the closet, tears flowed instantly. I got a new Kleenex box and filled up my water bottle. Water is important in this process because we lose so much when we are crying. I got a few big bags, and, one by one, I put things in them, and I cried. I kept going. As I filled each bag, I could feel the energy shifting. I put in his shoes and slippers. I put in his hats. It was gut wrenching and painful, but I was determined. I kept going. As I let each item drop into the bag, I honored the retrospections that came forward. I felt a deep appreciation and loving remembrance of the dear memories we had shared.

I put some of my own things in the bags too. Things I used to wear to school before I retired. I was not letting go of any part of the love we shared or the memories I held in my heart. Eckhart Tolle says attachment to things drops away by itself when you no longer seek to find yourself in them. I would not find Blaine or myself in these things. I would find him in my heart. I saved his shirts for pillows and one to use as a paint shirt. The paint shirt felt like a great way to make use of one of his shirts doing something I love, and my aunt gave me a pin from my grandma to pin on it as well. I purchased a widow bracelet so I could wear our rings on my wrist, and I kept a small box of mementos to revisit later.

My soul and spirit knew it was time to let go of Blaine's things. You will know when it is time too, and you will have your own way of doing it. A friend told me that when she let go of her husband's things, she asked her husband to direct the items to those who needed them. I took that advice. I said a special prayer that Blaine's things would be distributed in such a way that they would go to whomever needed them most.

The process of releasing is intimate and personal. I cannot tell you that this is the only way to let go, nor would I suggest a time frame in which to do it. None of this is easy, and it is an ongoing process—until it is not. No one knows the road ahead. No one can predict how the journey will unfold or how long it will take. If you still need to face the pain of letting go of your loved one's things, give yourself time and space to do what feels right for you. If you have been impatient with someone who struggles to let things go, I hope this helps you understand how difficult this process can be. A little compassion goes a long way.

Exercise:

- Below I include some suggestions and ideas for what to do to honor your loved one's things. What ideas resonate with you? What might be a first small step in your process of letting go?

    1. Create a memory box or display: Gather a collection of your loved one's belongings that represent their life and create a memory box or display. This might include photographs, letters, small trinkets, or any items that hold special meaning. It can serve as a tribute and a way to remember and honor their life. You might also label and document each item, including the stories and memories associated with them. This can be passed down to future generations to remember and connect with their family history.

    2. Repurpose or transform items: Consider repurposing or transforming some of their belongings into something new. For example, you could turn their clothing into a quilt or pillow, or create other artwork using their possessions. I used Blaine's clothing to create tree ornaments. This allows you to keep your loved one's memory alive.

    3. Create a memory book or album: Compile photographs, letters, and other mementos into a memory book or album. This can be a beautiful way to preserve their memory and share their life story with future generations.

    4. Incorporate their belongings into your daily life: Integrate some of their belongings into your daily routine. For example, you could use their favorite

coffee mug, wear their jewelry, or display their artwork in your home. This can create a sense of connection and keep their memory close.

5. Create a digital memorial: Build a website or online memorial page dedicated to your loved one. Include photos of them, their things, stories, and memories to share with family and friends.

6. Allow family members to choose an item: Put together some items that you are willing to let go to family members or close friends. Allow each member to choose one thing to keep in their memory. I remember doing this when we were cleaning my grandma and grandpa's house. We grandkids were allowed to take one thing. I chose a green water pitcher. It is very special to me.

Remember, there is no right or wrong way to let go of a loved one's belongings. Choose the methods that resonate with you and bring you comfort as you navigate the grieving process and honor your loved one's memory.

Tapping Exercise:

It is so important to be kind and compassionate to yourself during this task of letting go of your loved one's belongings. Our brains are wired to seek pleasure and avoid pain. If having to let go of the physical presence of our loved one is not enough, now it is up to us to let go of articles that are no longer useful. It can be daunting. But when you complete the task, it will bring some peace to your soul.

When tapping along with the following script, feel free to change the wording. The wording is to just keep you focused. You are tapping on the feelings and sending a signal to your brain that it is okay to feel a little calmer and more peaceful.

It is okay to process and release the many emotions you are experiencing.

Take a deep breath. Scan your body. Where does the dread of taking on another part of this grief journey reside? On a scale of 1-10, how intense is the feeling or emotion in your body right now, with 10 being most intense?

- Tapping on the side of the hand (the karate chop point), say the following words:

  Even though a part of me feels ready to tackle this task, another part of me just wants to hold on to each article. I am very kind to myself as I honor my feelings and love myself through this process. (Repeat three times.)

  - EB (Eyebrow): A part of me is ready to let go of some of these items.
  - SE (Side of the eye): Another part of me wants to keep all of them forever.
  - UE (Under the eye): Some days, seeing these items seems to make the pain worse.
  - UN (Under the nose): Some days, it feels like they give me comfort.
  - CH (Chin): Some say I should get the job done.
  - CB (Collarbone): Others say it's okay to wait.
  - UA (Under the arm): Sometimes, I feel confused, overwhelmed, and so sad.
  - TH (Top of the head): I'm choosing to believe I can do this as I choose the time that works best for me.

Take a deep breath. Check into how your body feels. Allow tears to come, yawn, or do whatever your body wants to do to release your emotions or tension. Any sign that your body is releasing is good. Then, continue tapping, using the script below.

- Tapping on the side of your hand (on the karate chop point), say:

Even though these articles have so many memories attached to them, I'm open to cherishing these memories. I'm open to gaining strength as I free the painful emotions I'm feeling right now. I love, honor, and accept myself and my feelings.

EB: A part of me has some fear of letting go of these things.

SE: I'm choosing to release this fear.

UE: A part of me is worried that I might regret some of my decisions.

UN: I'm choosing to release this worry.

CH: A part of me feels some doubt when making these decisions.

CB: I'm releasing this doubt along with the items that will be useful to others.

UA: A part of me is experiencing many emotions: extreme sadness, regret, anger.

TH: Another part of me feels ready to process and release the emotions that are holding me back. I'm choosing to release these painful feelings along with these many items.

Take a deep breath. Check in with your body and feel any changes. Then continue tapping.

- Tapping on the side of your hand (on the karate chop point), say:

Even though letting go is so difficult, I'm choosing to continue to release things and emotions whenever I feel it is good to do so. I'm open to feeling pain and peace at the same time. I'm open to becoming stronger as I experience all of these emotions. I'm honoring my loved one by taking actions that help me move forward and I do love, accept, and honor myself. (Repeat three times.)

EB: I'm choosing to release these items and painful emotions.

UE: I'm keeping the lessons and memories safe in my heart.

SE: I'm letting go of what is not needed, and I feel good about that.

UN: I'm feeling the love I want to keep in my heart.

CH: It feels safe to let go, to give to others.

CB: It feels safe to honor my loved one by taking care of myself.

UA: Right here and right now I feel safe.

TH: I'm choosing to feel peace and love as I continue to let go, and it feels good to do so.

Take a deep breath. Check in with your body and determine if the number you chose at the beginning of the tap has decreased. You may choose to do more rounds of tapping to lower the number.

If you are having difficulty with this, please consider working with a trained EFT practitioner, as they can customize the statements for exactly what you need.

Chapter 8

———

The Grieving Brain

Neuroscience and the Brain

Our brains sometimes have a hard time processing all the changes after a loss. It is helpful to understand what is happening in our brains when we lose our loved one.

When Blaine passed, I had a burning desire to get everything taken care of right away. When we put together all the arrangements for the celebration of life, a part of me wanted to choose the headstone at the same time and be finished. But it seemed we had been at the funeral home for a long time, and we had other things to deal with and prepare, and I decided to do it later. Then, there were a few hiccups, and the next thing I knew, it was September.

The fall weather was upon us, and I felt a sense of urgency creeping in. *I must deal with this! How can I leave his grave plot unmarked?* I have never been one to visit a gravesite. I always believed that a person's soul is not there, anyway. So why would I go there? We all have our own beliefs. Now it felt different. I learned some big lessons about life and death, and perhaps the initial shock had started to thaw. I was ready to find a nice marker for Blaine's gravesite.

Blaine had helped maintain two cemeteries. One was near our ranch up on Hillandale Road, and the other was in Val Marie. He and others volunteered to cut the lawn. It was something he felt was important, and looking back, it is one of the things I loved him for. Having a nice monument felt like something extra special I could do for him. *So, let's just do this! How hard can it be?* Little did I know, there was much to consider as I grappled with this decision. Through this experience, I learned something about how our brain reacts to change when we are in grief.

All I knew going into this task was that the marker should have a ranch theme. That seemed a given. When we were planning the celebration of life, Whitney had spotted a marker at the funeral home with a perfect ranch feel. I had an idea. I emailed Rick, one of the staff at the funeral home, and let him know what I was looking for. Once the design was ready, he sent me a draft. When I saw it, it took my breath away. The design was lovely, but seeing Blaine's name, and imagining it carved in that stone, made everything so real—shocking somehow. *This doesn't make any sense,* I thought. *I know he's gone! Why is seeing his name on this monument, almost a year after his death, overwhelming me like this?*

Recently, neuroscientists have released new information about what happens in the brain as we grieve. For example, Mary-Frances O'Connor's research on the grieving brain provides insight into how our brain functions after we lose a loved one. When we build a relationship with another person, she says, we develop neural pathways that solidify as time goes on. They become entrenched in our brain and make it comfortable and easy to be with that person. We know the person and their habits so well, often, we can determine what they will do next. We learn they will be there after work each day and that we will see them beside us each morning. In time, those same pathways create a virtual map of where you can expect your loved one to be. Blaine and I often knew what each other was thinking before we said it out loud.

When you lose a loved one, each time your brain looks for your person and does not find them, it tries to solve the problem, "Where they have gone?" It causes a yearning. This longing recurs until the brain map has updated itself. You wake up each morning realizing they are not there, and that realization repeats itself several times during the day.

Even when someone is no longer with you, you may have the impulse to reach out to them or expect to see them. Even though you know they are gone, your brain lags. It needs to adjust. I used the word "we" long after Blaine was gone. I said things like, "We have a seasonal spot in Cypress Hills" or "We have two children." It is not wrong if you think about your person as still being with you in spirit. But it can be misleading for those who do not know your story.

I remember counting myself as two people—if a server asked me how many seats I wanted for dinner at a restaurant, or if I was setting out plates for company at my place, I counted myself as two. It surprised me how difficult it was for my brain to readjust to the fact that I was now me, not "we," and one, not two.

While your brain is busy rewiring all these pathways, it makes sense that it becomes overloaded with thoughts, feelings, and emotions. This causes "grief brain," which affects your memory, concentration, and cognition. Maybe you cannot get much done, or maybe you forget things, and/or you walk around in a brain fog. Because these cognitive and emotional changes can occur, it is not advisable to make any major decisions during this time. Once I ordered Chinese food and gave the restaurant their phone number instead of mine. I did other things like that, too, but people just humored me. Had I not known about "grief brain," I would have thought I was going crazy.

As these neurological changes take place, many regions of your brain are playing a role in regulating your emotions. When neurochemicals and hormones flood your brain, they can cause symptoms such as sleep and appetite disturbances, or fatigue and anxiety. All these things are going on in the background while you are trying to carry out your regular, everyday tasks. These things slow down your mental processing, and that exhausts you. This is normal. The updating of the map takes time. We have to be patient with the process. Understanding what is happening is an important first step. Over time, as the brain builds new pathways and understandings, things get better. Do not rush it. Nurture yourself as you are going through this process.

After I understood this, I tried not to let my unexpected reactions to things take me to my knees. I realized: *It's just my brain trying to catch up.*

As for the monument, I found out there are multiple things to consider beyond the design. I needed to think through things like, "Do you want both your names put on the stone now, or do you want to wait and put your name on later? What size is your plot? Two plots or one? Double or single monument?" And there were questions I had to ask myself, like, "What if I should find another partner someday down the road? Then what happens? Do I still get buried next to Blaine?" It was not something Blaine and I had wanted to talk about, that is for sure. There are people who do this type of pre-planning. Perhaps it is not a bad idea. As for Blaine's monument, the design included cattle, a horse, a barn, cowboy boots, a rope, gloves, a fence post, and sheaves of wheat. It turned out beautifully!

Saying Goodbye

Goodbyes can be hard. Every fall since I can remember, when it was time to put the camper away after a summer of camping in the Cypress Hills, even though I knew there would be another season of camping next year, there was this enormous lump in my throat. I never knew what to do with it. Shutting the camper down for the season has always been sad, and the year after Blaine died, it was worse.

Every time we look to the future, we have to say goodbye to the past. This time, it was harder because everything had changed, and I did not know where I was headed. Nothing was certain. I was walking in what felt like an unknown world. We make plans for what we will do and how our lives will play out, but I have learned that plans must be flexible. At any moment, we can face something that will change everything. Sometimes we judge change as good or bad, right or wrong. It reminds me of a book I used to read to the kids at school called *That's Good! That's Bad!* by Margery Cuyler. In that book, every situation that was judged as good had a bad side to it and everything judged as bad had a good side to it. What a profound message: "If we look closely enough, there is more than one way of looking at every situation." As I have said before, deep down I know things in life happen for me, not against me. I believe there is a higher self that has a plan. My mind could not imagine how the loss of my husband, which was so awful, could ever result in anything good.

I have always seen myself as someone who embraces change. I find myself taking a hard look at the changes that have occurred since Blaine left. So much has happened, I can barely keep track of it all. There have been so many major life events: Whitney's wedding, becoming a grandparent, retiring, relocating, participating in online summits, creating a support community, and writing this book. I have traveled and developed new friendships and a vision for my future. I am learning to take life as it comes without judgment. I have realized I cannot label any of this. It just is. *Life is.* I can be sad about past events, or I can look back with fondness and joy. I can choose peace.

After I had hosted online grief summits and developed a list of contacts, I had the idea to send out an invitation through my email list to anyone who wanted to meet and be together, where we could hold a space in which our grief could be acknowledged and healing could take place. It turned out to be a special get-together. We heard each other's stories and took away some profound nuggets of wisdom from each other. These get-togethers continue to this day. One participant described grief as a portal, a door, or a gateway that lies before us, and ultimately, we choose to move through it. Or we can choose not to step through that gateway. I was thinking that when we try to go back, it prevents us from enjoying all the opportunities that lie on the other side of that portal. Our fear of moving through the portal makes us stay stuck in reliving the past. We can look back and regret what is over, or we can look back on memories as fuel that give us strength, courage, and the energy to move forward. Eventually, we learn to look back on memories with a smile, not feeling sad that they are over but feeling gratitude that they happened.

Our thoughts affect our emotions. It is natural to have sad thoughts, to feel helpless, and to despair over what was. When we turn toward the door that leads to the unknown, we do not know what lies ahead, and we get scared. Our minds go back to what we know, what felt comfortable. We resist. We get stuck in that loop. In the beginning, I felt this happening to me repeatedly. I would think about the future and, for a split second, get excited about what I might create. Then, I would get slammed back into fear and start thinking again about the past.

For me, the key was to recognize when it was happening. I asked myself, "Are these thoughts helpful to me?" If they weren't, I got curious. "What thoughts might be more helpful for me?" Writing my thoughts down and then speaking them aloud in my grief group helped. I was grateful to have a forum in which to share my thoughts with others who understood what I was going through. I am also grateful that in our group, there is a practice of giving and receiving. Sharing our grief with others can help us adopt a new mindset.

It all boils down to asking ourselves a couple of big questions. "What do I desire?" "Do I want my mind to continue to live in a past where I cannot bring myself to say goodbye, or do I want to continue to make new memories free of sadness and remorse?" "Do I want to step into a life of pure gratitude, joy, happiness, and love?"

In each moment, we have the power to choose what we want for our future. I remember at one point thinking:

I want to laugh again. I want to laugh so hard the tears run down my face and I cannot stop. I want to feel free. Free from the suffering of the past and free from any negative thoughts. To do that, I have to let the past go. I must surrender to the suffering, the pain, the loss, and the fear. I must embrace the memories from my past, cherish them, use them to fuel my future, and step bravely through that portal. That's my choice. Thanks to the many people who walk with me in this world and in the spirit world, I don't have to do it alone. The beautiful thing is that, in my mind, I can envision Blaine along with all my other guides and angels, walking ahead of me. They are shining a light so I can see, comforting me when needed, and encouraging me to say goodbye to what was, to continue moving forward, trusting that the road ahead of me will unfold beautifully. I believe they are excited to show me the way there.

I believe you, too, have guides, ancestors, and loved ones cheering you on. They want you to find your joy. Surrender to the path, whatever that may be.

The Firsts

One of the toughest things I have found in dealing with my grief is facing what we refer to as the "firsts." I did not understand the firsts until I lost Blaine. It is not just the first Christmas, Thanksgiving, or birthday. It is more than that. It is the first time you eat in a restaurant alone, camp alone, travel alone, walk alone, sleep alone, or buy groceries alone. Every time you experience something for the first time without your loved one, it has its own thoughts and emotions attached. It is overwhelming. It is exhausting.

The firsts are complex, incomprehensible, gut-wrenching experiences. Each time we encounter a first, we relearn how to do that experience without our loved one. This is the premise of Mary-Frances O'Connor's book *The Grieving Brain*. New traditions, memories, and neurological patterns are being formed through these firsts, and something is always going to come up emotionally. It is an enormous challenge.

The firsts do not just happen in the first year. Sometimes firsts take place years later. Some experiences do not happen that often. For example, I will not need to buy a car for a few years. The first time I go shopping for one without Blaine will be a first. We might even avoid certain experiences for a time, as they are too painful. We will face them when we are ready.

To transform the pain, for me it was best to face the firsts head on. Some firsts you can see coming. You can plan for them. But some will surprise you. When emotions welled up inside, I tried not to resist. I did my best to feel them, be patient with them, and sit with them. I have learned from experience that getting busy is not a long-term solution. It only masks the pain. Ignoring or pushing down the pain will stall the inevitable—and holding that beach ball of emotion under the water is exhausting!

As I noted earlier, make a point of mourning. Cry, write, draw, talk, listen to music, punch a pillow, run or walk, meditate, take a bath, do yoga, or get help from a therapist, coach, or healer. Do whatever feels right for you. Make the time sacred. I felt better when I let go of resistance to something, and the next time I experienced that thing, it was easier. I could feel when my emotions were building and ready to bubble over, and then I found ways to release them before they became overwhelming.

After releasing the emotion, it is important to fill the gap left from your release. I asked my coach once, "Why am I feeling so empty inside? I am doing the work to release the emotion." My coach reminded me I was not filling myself up again with things I enjoy. So, find things you love to do, things you can look forward to, or things you can do to help others. These will fill the emptiness.

When I did the work to let go of the pain of the firsts, I gave myself room energetically to feel more of the essence of Blaine. Opening up and allowing that energy to flow brought me to a stronger, honoring, loving connection with him. Hope for a new, joyful life emerged as I navigated the gap between the world before my loss and the world after it. I did my best to make commitments for the future. No matter what, I will never forget Blaine. He will always be there loving me through all the firsts and beyond as I continue my new journey.

Journal Exercises:

1. Can you rekindle what lights you up inside? Spending time in nature, crafting, gardening, cooking, and spending time with family and friends helped fill my cup. What will help you fill your cup?

2. Try this meditation:

    Take a few deep breaths. Close your eyes. Imagine deep roots going down into the earth from your feet. Then imagine a white light shining down on you from above. Allow the light to penetrate your whole body. Imagine a happy moment when you were little. What kinds of things did you play with? Did you sing? Did you color? Did you like to dance? Get curious about those things you did. How might you recreate those opportunities now? If your mind is telling you that you can't, just let it be. Keep thinking about what small things you might do that would bring you joy. Maybe there is a class you would like to take. Perhaps there is volunteer work you would love to do. Maybe it is as simple as finding time to color or draw. By being curious, you are planting a seed. You might not get the insight right away. Continue to focus on your breath for a few minutes in silence. When you are ready, open your eyes. Write down any thoughts, feelings, or ideas that came to mind (no matter what they were). Repeat this meditation as often as you like. Be patient with yourself and the process.

3. Yawn a few times.

    When we yawn, it stimulates the muscles in the back of the mouth and throat and it stimulates the vagus nerve. An article by multi-faith educator Sarah Bowen in *Spirituality + Health* offers twelve reasons we should yawn every day.[14] Yawning:

    a. stimulates alertness and concentration,
    b. optimizes brain activity and metabolism,
    c. improves cognitive function,
    d. increases memory recall,
    e. enhances consciousness and introspection,
    f. lowers stress,
    g. relaxes every part of our body,
    h. improves voluntary muscle control,
    i. enhances athletic skills,
    j. fine-tunes our sense of time,
    k. increases empathy and social awareness, and
    l. enhances pleasure and sensuality.

After you have tried stimulating the vagus nerve this way, take note of how it changes the way you feel. Try writing some of the things you have been thinking about and then yawning with the intention to release any emotional energy that may be causing you stress or discomfort.

Chapter 9

Holidays and Special Days

Holidays

Holidays and special days can be so difficult for those in grief. The memories are so strong because special days come with emotion. Brain research shows we remember events more clearly when they are associated with a heightened emotion. One well-known study that supports this idea is the flashbulb memory study conducted by Brown and Kulik in 1977.[15]

They are referred to as "flashbulb memories" because they are as if a photograph was taken of the event. After Blaine passed, every holiday changed for me. I would think back to the fun we had as a family, whether we were traveling or just spending time with each other. We were always together for the holidays. Now, because he was not there, I found the special days uncomfortable, not exciting or joyful in the way they had been in the past. Blaine passed away on October 26. His birthday was on October 27, the same day as Mom's. The first year, those days were spent just getting through the initial shock. I was preparing for the celebration of life and leaning on the support of friends and family. I was numb. So, the following year was more like a first for me for his birthday (and, of course, for his death anniversary). My friend Judy came to stay with me that year. It was nice to have a plan. She told me, "Angela, if you want to change your mind at the last minute, I will not come, but I will be here for you." I will never forget this gesture. She did come, and we went in and out of the shops around town and out for lunch. It felt good to have her there.

Halloween arrived only five days after Blaine passed. I had put up the Halloween decorations at the beginning of the month and had put a lot of time into them. It was a creative outlet for me, and I enjoyed it. On October 31, I put on a brave face and gave out candy to all the kids who came to the door. I did not have to do this—and it might even seem crazy that I did. But when we had lived out on the ranch, we did not get trick or treaters, so in our new home in Maple Creek, this was my first opportunity to have fun with the kids. My family was staying with me, so that was helpful. That night I wrote in my journal:

Blaine would have loved giving out candy to the kids. We had 210! He would have teased them, and they would have loved it. I feel like the whole rug has been ripped out from under my feet.

So, even though I was filled with sadness, I could enjoy something at the same time. This is the beauty of our human selves. If we allow it, we can hold more than one emotion. I wanted to do this, and, rather than let my sadness hold me down, I allowed myself, with the support of my family, to grab as much joy out of the moment as I could. It also was a distraction at a time when my brain was overwhelmed with all that had happened.

I am so glad I took a few days to head back to Val Marie before the first Christmas. We all gather every other year for Christmas, and as it worked out, this was the year for Blaine's side of the family to all be together. Blaine's nephew Rick and his wife Deanna hosted. Having spent a couple days back home after the celebration of life helped me to resolve some of the shock of no longer living there, working there, or having Blaine with me. With that behind me, I was more able to concentrate on Christmas with Blaine's family.

I suppose Christmas went as well as I could have expected, considering how fresh my grief was. I had learned about being present in the moment from Eckhart Tolle, and that was helping me a great deal. In my journal, I wrote:

Anytime I felt sad, I felt for Blaine in my energy field. I knew he was there and then I concentrated on being in the present moment.

I had to keep my thoughts focused on what was happening at the moment. The smell of the turkey, the conversation with family, and the taste of the amazing food kept me focused in the present moment. I was able to enjoy the time with Blaine's family despite my grief. I also had my "granddog" to hold on Christmas morning. Lewis is a papillon and poodle cross, otherwise known as a "papi-poo." He belongs to Curtise and Jen. There is something about having a pet on your lap to comfort you and keep your mind in the present. A couple of friends took me for a drive to see the Christmas lights around town. I especially love the ambience at Christmas, and seeing all the lights prompted me to put a few up in my own room. They gave off a warm glow that made me feel comfortable and safe.

Easter was interesting. It was just the kids and me. Normally Blaine's family would have been together for Easter. Blaine and I often hosted Easter at the ranch because Easter was calving season for us. Hosting the event meant that we could stay home and check on the cows during the day. This year, we went to Curtise's house, and he cooked a stuffed roast. Like I did every year, I brought chocolate bunnies for the kids. We also ate a lot of mini eggs. We all love those!

Whitney and Sheldon also had a new puppy named Bentley, an Australian shepherd toy—so his mannerisms are a lot like our Patches', but Bentley is smaller. We watched a movie, went for a walk to the park with the dogs together as a family, and played games. Later in the day, we ordered wings from the local hotel. It was way outside our usual tradition, but I realized that we were finding what worked for us. Some moments were sad for me when I thought about Blaine not being there. It felt messy, like a trial-and-error technique. I do not think any of us knew how to approach these days, so we were open to trying new things to see what worked. We persevered, and at the end of the day, I decided we would be okay. We would have to be patient. We could come up with a plan as a family for future holidays.

As I created new patterns for firsts and holidays, I gained courage, and knew I would be strong enough to face other firsts in the future. I knew I would survive. I knew what I needed, and I knew how to take care of myself.

Special Days

Mother's Day was one of those holiday tsunamis of grief that came out of nowhere. I thought it would be okay. After all, I survived Christmas and Easter. Mother's Day, however, was the worst of the worst for me. It marked a turning point in my grief. It was the beginning of a good hard look at the road ahead of me. I remember Blaine used to joke, "Every day is Mother's Day." I would groan, and he would give me that grin of his. He loved to tease. He especially liked it if he could get a rise out of you. It was entertaining for him if you retaliated in some way. His jokes and teasing were all in fun. It is something I really miss. The picture I have of him that I used for the celebration of life has this grin.

The thing is, he always found a way to make my Mother's Day special. Sometimes he gave me flowers, maybe a bundle of crocuses, which are one of my favorites. Sometimes he made a special supper; other years we would go out for a meal. The kids, Blaine, and I were all together. I remember fondly us going out with our friends to the Val Marie Hotel for wings or a Mother's Day buffet. The hotel had a Western feel to it. The walls had wood paneling, local art, and pictures of some of the local people from the community. There was a jukebox and a pool table. A small dance floor and stage were corralled off with wooden posts. People would come from neighboring towns like Frontier, Climax, Ponteix, or Mankota. It was a time to see people and visit and, of course, a time for Blaine to tell stories and joke around with everyone. We enjoyed laughing and visiting.

Blaine and I would go home full and happy and discuss all the evening's events. I did not realize how important that was for me and how I enjoyed the special attention Blaine gave me. I was surprised how hard this wave of grief hit me. In hindsight, it was more than that—it was a reckoning with my soul. My mind kept going back to how it used to be, to the past, to what I was missing, to my future without Blaine. I know now that reliving the past and yearning for what is lost for the future causes much suffering.

I questioned my existence, everything I believed in. "Is there really a God?" "Are there really angels, guides, and helpers?" "What if it is all a lie?" This intense pain continued off and on, right into Father's Day in June. I was furious with God and in a dark place emotionally. I was experiencing a dark night of the soul, and it continued for several nights. A "dark night" is a crisis of faith in a difficult, painful period in life. Some people say it comes before revelation. You have no choice but to surrender to the pain. It is scary, dark, dramatic, and awful. The following is a post from my journal about my dark night of the soul. Understand that this is what I wrote after a lot of mourning. I was crying at my guides, yelling at the angels, at God, and at anyone I thought might listen.

Tonight, the discomfort continues. I dream about how much fun and joy Blaine and I would be having living so close to the kids and Cypress. We would be travelling and enjoying life and it would be so easy. This is so hard. Every day is so difficult. I open the cupboard under the altar, and there's the Othello board. I'm brought to tears instantly. I played that game with him on the bed when he was sick. We turned the TV on in the room and watched the Rider game (football) and ate peas in the pod that I got from the market. It was all I could think of to do with him. It was fun in its own way. I tried so hard to stay positive and strong. I'm so tired of the effort staying afloat in this new life requires. There's no comfort like before, and I cannot go back. I'm backed up against the wall, and there's only one way out, and it's taking me further away from what I knew. I just cry and then sit and stare.

I remember thinking there was no way out of the pain. I felt stuck. It was like being stuck in a dark tunnel and not seeing a way out. It was a horrible feeling, yet I learned it is a beautiful place to be because it is the place where awakening is born. This is the place of surrendering to what was so you can look at what lies ahead. Like I said, to open ourselves up to something new, we have to let go of the old. This was difficult and scary, but, thankfully, I had support. With the energy healers' spiritual guidance and my grief coach's practical advice, I navigated through this time.

Between Mother's Day and Father's Day, I got many messages and signs from Blaine. I was busy interpreting and following the breadcrumbs spirit provided for me. (I will describe more in the section on signs and messages later.) As I look back now, I was opening more and more to spirit. I was taking the pain and transforming the powerful energy into healing and helping others. I created my blog and my online grief summit, and I found more ways to be joyful. I embraced time with family and walks in nature, and my love of music helped to lift my vibration. I was allowing myself to be happy instead of trying to resist a future without Blaine. I wrote:

Each day I get a little farther from the life behind me and closer to the life ahead of me.

I was at a crossroads, a turning point, and I was seeing that since there was no turning back, I must move forward.

My grandson, Benson Blaine, was born just before Father's Day. Curtise was born on June 15, and Benson was born June 16. I was filled with joy to meet Benson, and a part of my heart broke at the same time. Looking back, I felt ashamed and guilty for feeling the way I did. I remember talking to people and saying, "I am so excited." But I had a feeling in the pit of my stomach, knowing that was not the complete truth.

Blaine would have loved being a grandpa. He would have been over-the-moon excited to see Benson and he would have spent so much time with him. He loved babies, and he loved kids. He knew intuitively how to connect with them. I wanted to share this with him so badly. I did not know how to tell people how I was feeling. *What kind of grandma am I to not have the absolute joy that all grandmas feel when they get to hold their first grandchild?*

One day, one of my friends said, "I am sure that even though this is an exciting time, it must be really hard too." That acknowledgement was huge! It gave me permission to feel excited and sad. Being acknowledged in our grief is so important for healing.

On July 11, Sheldon and Whitney had their traditional wedding ceremony with family and friends. Even though they were already officially married, it felt like we needed to have a celebration. As mother of the bride, you have specific duties as traditional weddings go, and one of those is to give the welcome-to-the-family speech for the groom. It was a source of great pride for me to welcome Sheldon and the union of our two families. But I had an underlying sadness in having to do it alone. It seemed unfair not to have Blaine beside me.

The human part of me yearned to have him here in the physical. The comfort we had built over our thirty-five years together was missing. The spiritual part of me, however, knew he was there. I felt his presence as I went about my daily tasks. I had to process the emotion around the event for my human self and show myself the patience and compassion I deserved. I knew if I did not deal with the emotion, I would not be able to enjoy the wedding. If you do not let the sadness go, you cannot feel the joy the same way. It is like sadness can occupy so much space, there is no room for any other emotion. So, I processed and released the sadness in the evenings by journaling, and it also helped me get the sleep I needed.

Another thing that had to change was my way of thinking. The focus needed to be on Sheldon and Whitney and their special day. It was not about me, yet I had to be careful to take care of myself so I could be available to them in a helpful way. I chose to approach the whole thing in that context. Instead of thinking about how unfair it was to not have Blaine here, I thought about what I needed to do to make the event the best it could be. It was fun to sit down with Sheldon and Whitney and go through what needed to be done and the vision they had for the day. We made lists.

We divided and conquered. It was fun to see how their vision unfolded so perfectly.

In the end, it warmed my heart to see everyone smiling and dancing and, especially, to see Whitney and Sheldon enjoying themselves and embracing their day. Blaine's picture was on the table, and under it there was a message, "We know you would be here today if heaven were not so far away." People signed their names.

Yes, there were tears. In my speech, I talked about Blaine and what he would say and think on this special occasion. I rehearsed it, hoping I could do it without tears, but I knew that if I cried, it would be okay. I did not put any pressure on myself. Of course I was nervous. I was proud I could make this speech for the kids. Before they were engaged, Sheldon had officially asked Blaine for his blessing. Blaine had so much respect for Sheldon. Blaine thought the world of Sheldon and Whitney and would have been so delighted about the entire event.

I missed Blaine's ability to coordinate people and assign or delegate jobs. He was so good at that. I believe he was there the whole way through, guiding and supporting us in ways that I probably do not even know.

A few days before the wedding, as I was running an errand, three mourning doves flew erratically in front of the windshield of my car. (Yes, they are called "mourning" doves, as opposed to "morning" doves, which makes them even more special to me.) The symbolism of a mourning dove is that it brings messages from loved ones who have passed to spirit. Mourning doves mate for life. They symbolize persistence, finding beauty in the darkest of situations, and carrying on in difficult times. They represent sticking by someone's side no matter what, letting go of the past, and moving forward. Mourning doves bring the message that love energy never dies; it just transforms into something new. The tears run down my cheeks when I think of all the beautiful messages that come from that bird and its song. It felt like they were a sign telling me to slow down and have a giggle amidst all the business. The next day, out in my front yard, there were butterflies flying around my big pine tree. This happened for the two days leading up to the wedding and on the day of. It has not happened since. Butterflies are a metaphor for transformation, hope, rebirth, and resurrection, and for the triumph of the spirit and the soul. They were a reminder for me to trust in the journey and the process of healing and to keep going inward for answers and the guidance. As long as I stay connected to my higher self and keep moving forward, I can see magic and miracles happen every day.

If you are grieving, and the holidays are near, I suggest you feel into the feelings that might come up for you around the event a few days ahead of time. Tune into your thoughts around the day and allow any emotion to come up. Acknowledge it. Then release it by writing, crying, talking to someone, or being present with it in your own way. If you can, before the day comes, release some of the energy, anxiety, and anticipation. Make sure you are eating properly and getting rest. Self-care is important when we are grieving, especially around these special days. I like to have a plan and set an intention for the day. You can have a Plan A and a backup Plan B and C available, if that feels right. In the end, if you do none of those and choose something else, it is okay. It is the process of planning that helps.

In 2023, for my birthday, I planned to go to a movie. I decided it was my special day, and I needed to make it fun. I had a hair appointment in the morning and then went to Medicine Hat to the cinema. Blaine loved going to the movies—he especially loved the popcorn. We did not like the same movies, but we humored each other. I chose a comedy. I was excited about my decision and enjoyed it. We need to have this kind of foresight for special days. I knew I was covered, I had a plan I knew would bring me joy, something I could look forward to, and I did not have to wait for others to plan for me. I was in control.

If your plan involves others, ask them well ahead of time. Let them know you need them so you are not disappointed because disappointment can throw you into negative thinking. I did not have as much planned for our anniversary, the day after my birthday. It was sad, and that was okay. Perhaps next year I will plan something that will extend over both days.

It is important to take responsibility for your special days. Sometimes they do not turn out the way you expect, but if that happens, it is an opportunity to discover what does not work for you. Only you know what feels right. Even an evening at home can be meaningful if you make it special.

In the same year, 2023, I hosted Easter dinner for Blaine's family. The first year without Blaine, the kids and I were alone at Curtise's house. I decided to host the dinner at my place and invite Blaine's family. It was the first time for me to host this number of people in my own home without Blaine. It was an honor to do so, and it felt good, but I missed Blaine. He always looked after the logistics, like where everyone would sit. I was hosting in my new, smaller place so I did not know how it would work, but we made it work. The kids came and helped, and I was proud of myself and them.

Each time I tackle a first, I get clearer: *What brings me joy? What doesn't bring me joy?* I gain insight into how I want to move forward. It becomes easier for me to accept and embrace the new and let go of the old.

Once I got to know my pattern when it came to firsts, I developed confidence. I knew what to do. I knew I would survive because I had done it before. I knew the emotions would be strong, but they would pass as I allowed them to surface. Now I have the courage to face whatever firsts might be still to come. I have developed an important skill that will help me for the rest of my life.

Exercise:

- If you are grieving, and the holidays are near, I suggest you make a plan and feel into the feelings that might come up for you. Use the questions below as your guide.

Journal Questions:

- What is the next occasion I want to be prepared for? What kinds of memories come up around this event? Describe in detail. What specifically do I want to honor and remember about my loved one on this occasion? What will bring meaning to this event and honor my loved one at the same time? (See idea starters below.) How can I make this easy for myself? How can I take extra-special care of myself at this particular time?

Call to Action:

- Make a plan for your next "first" or holiday occasion. I am including a list that may help you with this process.
  1. Light a candle. This is a simple thing you can do that does not create a lot of fuss. It can be a symbol of your loved one's presence and can bring warmth and comfort.
  2. When you get together with others, share stories and memories. At first, some people may feel uncomfortable sharing. That is okay. You can share your memories. As you do this, it gives

others permission to do the same. You can do this spontaneously in conversation or set aside a special time. Whatever feels right for you and your situation is best.

3. Cook their favorite dish. Blaine loved carrot cake! I love to take carrot cake muffins to family gatherings. Our daughter's wedding cake was made with carrot cake. My niece made it. It makes the event that much more special, and it is a fun way to honor their memory and celebrate their life.

4. Donate to a cause in their name. Finding a cause that was important to your loved one can make this meaningful.

5. Write a letter to your loved one. Express your feelings, share updates, or simply write about how much you miss them. You could even start a journal dedicated completely to them, documenting your thoughts and memories.

6. Start a new tradition. For reasons described in this chapter, I think going to movies might become a tradition for me on my birthday and/or anniversary. It might also be a movie night at home. It feels right. Is there something your loved one enjoyed that holds significance in your relationship? This new tradition can create a sense of connection.

7. Perform acts of kindness. Engage in activities your loved one would have appreciated. Perform acts of kindness or volunteer for a cause in their memory. This can be a way to honor their values.

8. Plant a memorial garden or plant their favorite flowers or plants. In our last spring together, Blaine came to the greenhouse with me. He fell in love with one arrangement because of the lavender in the

center of the pot. I have incorporated lavender into my outside flower bed and also into my logo.

9. Listen to their favorite music. Play the songs your loved one enjoyed, or that you enjoyed together. Music is powerful and has a way of evoking memories and emotions. Music can help you feel connected to your loved one.

10. Write a poem. The night before Blaine's birthday this past year, I felt compelled to write a poem about him. I do not usually write poems, but that evening, it just felt right. It was not perfect, but it felt good to share my thoughts. I shared it on my personal Facebook page the next day. It felt like a fitting tribute.

Remember, there is no right or wrong way to honor and remember a loved one. There is just your way! It has to be meaningful to you. Reach out for support and more ideas.

Chapter 10

Signs, Messages, and God Winks

Messages from Our Loved Ones

We all have intuition and the ability to tap into it. We get signs and guidance from our angels, the universe, God, or a higher power (whatever that is for you). We can also get messages from our loved ones who have crossed over. You might feel that while others can get messages and inspiration from their loved ones in spirit, you simply cannot. Getting messages from your loved one is about paying attention, trusting, and having faith in something bigger than you. You have to be willing to open up your heart to the possibility, be mindful of the subtle signs that come into your awareness, and then acknowledge when you do receive a message. Like learning any new skill, it takes practice.

Even when we recognize our ability to get messages, we can get caught up in our lives and forget. I am sure you have a story, or you know someone who has received messages or signs from above. We can dismiss these things as coincidences, yet we know intuitively that the whole event was orchestrated. We are never alone.

Sometimes our loved ones in spirit arrange delightful surprises for us. Maybe a friend shows up at the right time or a situation turns out better than we had planned. I like the song by Garth Brooks where he talks about "Unanswered Prayers." The lyrics are about how sometimes we pray for things, and then, when it seems our prayers go unanswered, we were disappointed. Over time, however, we discover that the original plan would not have been the best for us. Sometimes there is something better around the corner and we do not know it. Everything in life is happening for you, but sometimes, it is hard to see this. I think our loved ones are trying to give us encouragement, and we need confirmation that they are not far away. They help shore up our faith when we most need it. I know friends who receive signs in the form of feathers, coins, and heart-shaped rocks. Sometimes we get messages in our dreams, from something a friend says, or in a song we hear on the radio. The signs can also come from animals, repeating numbers, or a message on a billboard.

When my grandmother passed away, many members of my family started to see dimes appearing here and there. The dimes seem to show up at times we needed a sign from the spirit world the most. I remember Grandma sent me a dime in the waiting room of the hospital, when I was waiting for Blaine to go in for hip surgery. A nervous wreck, I found a dime lying right at my feet—that was no accident. Grandma was there with us. When Blaine and I were going through challenges and we needed to move, the dimes started coming. At one critical time in my grief, I found one right at my feet as I was going into our garage. I have saved all Grandma's dimes—I have collected seven since moving to Maple Creek. The feeling I get when I discover a dime is the confirmation that it is from Grandma. The timing and place let me know it is no accident it is there.

My Aunt Sharon has great stories about dimes she has found from my grandmother too. Grandma leaves them in unusual places. One dime was in a teapot at the back of Sharon's camper trailer. Sharon never actually used the tea pot. When she was cleaning out the trailer to sell, she found it way in the back. The tea pot was dusty and needed washing, and when she opened the lid, she found a Canadian dime inside. She had bought the teapot at Goodwill in the United States. That Canadian dime had no business in that teapot!

Another dime was under the dishpan in the sink of her motor home. Sharon emptied that dishpan once or twice a day. She finds dimes behind pictures on a shelf when she is dusting and on the windowsill when washing windows.

One night, Sheldon and Whitney turned the TV off after an evening of playing PlayStation. They woke up in the morning to the TV blaring. Even if the cat had stepped on the remote to turn the TV on, he could not have turned it onto the satellite. Western movies were one of Blaine's favorite types of movies to watch. That was what was blaring on the TV.

Another time, in the wee hours of the morning on October 27 (Blaine's birthday), Jen was working the night shift at the hospital. A TV in an unoccupied room turned on and was blaring. Then, when she went down the hallway to shut it off, another TV was on as well. She messaged me in the morning to tell me she was sure it was Blaine playing tricks.

One of my special signs is a bird that seems to sing just for me. Its song is intriguing—and incessant. At first, I thought it was an owl. I like birds and I notice birds singing, but I have never been an avid bird watcher, and never paid attention to any one birdsong. For no apparent reason, this song caught my attention. I noticed it when I was going on walks, when I was sitting in reflection, when I was crying, and often, when I was writing my blog. When I went on my trip to Europe, it continued. I heard it when I was exploring the forest in Germany and touring around Switzerland. It haunted me. *What type of bird was it?* So, I listened to bird calls on the internet. I got my grandmother's book of bird calls out. I had gifted her a book called *The Bird Songs Anthology: 200 Birds from North America and Beyond*, which included an audio player. You could just push a button to listen to the call of each of the 200 species. I listened to many, but I could not find it.

One day, I was venting into my journal (as I sometimes do). I wrote with some frustration, as the bird was singing outside. *What the heck kind of bird is that?* Later, I googled "birds that sound like an owl" and discovered the bird is a mourning dove.

It was not long after that discovery that I noticed another bird's song. It was similar in tone to the mourning dove yet not the same. It went on for several weeks. I went to Vancouver Island, and it serenaded me there too. I asked different people what they thought it was. I even downloaded an app to my phone so I could record the bird and have it analyzed. It never worked. One day, as I was going through bird songs randomly on YouTube, I found it.

This one is a Eurasian collared dove, which explains why it was so similar—they are both doves.

When I looked up the symbolism for doves, I found they represent the soul of someone who has passed making a smooth and peaceful transition. They assure us that, no matter what is happening, peace will always follow. They can mean new beginnings and adventures are waiting for us, and that we are looked after, watched over, and have the power to get things done. They represent love, compassion, fidelity, understanding, and generosity in a relationship. They symbolize a love for words and a path to bring peace to the world with your words. That is beautiful messaging. When I hear these doves now, I listen and know intuitively that I'm not alone. I am on the right path. I am at peace.

Mediumship

Blaine loved talking to people in this life. He had a gift for being able to start a conversation with anyone about anything. It seems fitting that he loves connecting with others still. When I work with healers, often he shows up to deliver messages to me through them. He has managed to get messages to me directly too. The first time this happened was through a synchronicity of events.

Just over a month after Blaine transitioned, I was on my way to Val Marie to visit family and friends. It was my first visit since his celebration of life and my first trip alone. In the morning of the day I was set to head down there, I heard Blaine's voice yell, "Ange!" I was startled out of sleep, and it felt urgent that I get up and get going. I guess he was excited about me heading home. He had plans for me. He was making sure I got on my way in good time.

I planned to stay at my nephew's house in Val Marie for a few days. I got a phone call from a Val Marie friend, Twila, a spiritual healer who has a background in shamanic healing. She asked, "Do you want to walk the labyrinth with me?" I was surprised but intrigued and accepted her invitation. I had never walked a labyrinth before. There was a labyrinth built in 2017 by Susan Howard and Neil Ward, owners of some lovely vacation suites in the Grasslands National Park known as "The Crossing." This one, Mary's Labyrinth, is the first legacy labyrinth in Canada. Legacy labyrinths are physically and energetically connected around the world to one another, forming an energetic network to promote global healing and understanding. I knew Twila would have walked the labyrinth many times and she would be a great person to guide me through the experience. This was not the first time she had helped our family with spiritual guidance.

We experienced some strange activity just before our family moved from our home on Hillandale Road to the home place where Blaine had grown up. We had recently put the place up for sale with a real estate agent. Lights switched on and off by themselves. Patches was looking off into space and tilting his head as though someone were there. Also, a door to the attic in the old shop kept opening. The attic door was heavy, and each time Blaine had to move it back, he wondered how it could have moved on its own. One day, we went to town for supper, but before we left, I had the kids clean their rooms in the basement. I wanted to keep everything neat and clean just in case someone came to look at the house. When we came back, the basement bedrooms had been messed up. The sheets were off the beds; the pillows were on the floor. We were worried and afraid. I called Twila, and she came out and talked to the spirit living there.

Apparently, this spirit had been watching over us. Twila told us things this spirit had done to protect us during the time we were living there. For example, one afternoon, there had been a fire near our farmhouse that we did not realize was happening. An aerosol can had ended up in the burn barrel. It blew up and caused a grass fire. That fire went around our shop building and burned around the perimeter of the stack of highly flammable hay bales. It seems impossible, but that is what happened. That fire could have burned out of control.

Also, once the motor on our vehicle went out for no good reason. It was a newer vehicle under warranty. We never did understand why. Twila said our spirit person had been protecting us from a potential accident. Twila helped us understand that the reason this spirit was making all the fuss and mess in the house was because we were planning to move. This spirit had been quietly with us while we lived there without us knowing for many years and now was upset that we would be leaving her there alone. Twila helped our family and the spirit through that transition to move on. Even though I didn't know it at the time, she would help me in starting the journey moving forward, this time in my grief.

On the day we were to go walk the labyrinth, Twila came to pick me up, and I jumped in the truck. She explained why she was there: "Blaine came to me in spirit. I was just stepping out of the house to go feed the horses, and there he was. He told me I had to take you to walk the labyrinth. That is why I called you. I did not know what I would do if you said no. He seemed pretty persistent." She told me I would be okay—that even in my grief, I was whole. I was not broken. Cathleena told me that too. I wondered what it meant because at the time I felt pretty broken.

I walked Mary's Labyrinth, intending to try to make sense of it all. I remember very little about the walk to the middle of the labyrinth, but I remember sitting down on the rock in the middle and feeling the energy ground me. I felt a peace come over me. When I walked out, I sat on another rock, facing west. I stared at the pinky-blue sky. Twila said that facing west meant I was comfortable and living in the now, in the present moment. It all felt meaningful and beautiful. It made the day special, and I never forgot that encounter. I was grateful for what Blaine and Twila had done for me.

I have always been curious about healing, healers, energy, and how it all works. Sometimes healers I had connected with online had specials or free sessions, so I took advantage of those opportunities to get information about how they accessed the spirit world. Each time I found a new energy healer or astrologer, it was divinely guided and timed. I always got the information I needed. Over time, I understood that it was my higher self drawing these experiences to me. Each time I felt the urge to connect with a new healer, I simply said yes.

Mediums are psychics who communicate with those in the spirit world. You may have heard of the famous Hollywood Medium, Tyler Henry. Other well-known mediums include Mark Anthony, Colette Baron-Reid, and Lisa Williams. They have gifts of being able to bring evidential information from loved ones who have crossed over. Evidential mediums provide specific and verifiable information (evidence) about the spirit person's identity, personality, or experiences.

The first evidential medium I worked with was Melinda Vail. One day, long after I had interviewed her on my first summit, I got an email from her assistant saying Melinda would like to do a free session with me. Wow! At that point, Melinda was booked months in advance, but somehow she had an opening on October 27, the day of Blaine's and Mom's birthdays. I knew I was meant to take that session.

The week before, I was going through a box and found a *TeleMiracle Telethon* teddy bear I had received in recognition of a donation I had made to TeleMiracle in honor of Blaine's aunt. I decided to put that teddy bear on my bed because one of the speakers in my summit had suggested having a teddy bear on your bed can bring comfort at nighttime. I had not had a teddy bear on my bed since I was a teenager. One of the first things Melinda mentioned in her reading was that teddy bear on my bed.

The day Melinda did the reading on Zoom, my friend Judy was there. I was in my office with the door closed during the session. Melinda said Judy was rubbing her arm. Indeed, Judy had just gone for some treatment for the muscles in her arm and later confirmed she had been rubbing it. Melinda also named off names that I had already interviewed for my next summit, as well as friends and family who were close to Blaine and me.

Mediumship may not be for everyone, but it provided me with great comfort. It is not the only way Blaine chose to communicate with me. Once Blaine showed up when I was meeting with a numerologist. She did not do mediumship normally, so it was a shock for her when Blaine appeared with a message for me. That is typical of Blaine—I am sure he got a kick out of surprising her.

I am taking classes on mediumship because I find it interesting that we all have the divine gift to communicate with the spirit world in our own unique ways. Since I started taking classes, I can ask Blaine questions and the answers come to me as a knowing. I have asked him questions in my journal and have received answers through channeled writing, and I talk to him and hear answers in my mind.

There are many ways we can get messages from our loved ones in spirit through our senses of sight, taste, smell, hearing, feeling, and knowing. These are called our "clairs." The information comes subtly, and at first we barely recognize it. The biggest hurdle I have found to expanding my mediumship is that my mind finds it difficult to believe it is possible to communicate with the spirit world. But if we can sit patiently in stillness, raise our vibration to one of gratitude, love, trust, and faith, in time, a message will come. The more we take time to practice this skill, the better we will get.

Often, we dismiss intuitive messages as coincidence. Our minds get in the way and talk us out of believing these things are real. We tend to think it is our imagination. As I work more and more with my spiritual connection, I realize that imagination really is a playground for exploring psychic connection. The imagination realm is where psychic mediumship can thrive and unfold. Imagination can foster a sense of wonder, curiosity, and openness to the spiritual realm. When I am practicing mediumship, it allows me to explore and expand my beliefs and perspectives beyond what my mind thinks is rational. I share ideas and symbols that come to me, no matter how crazy they might seem to my mind. I am learning that as I practice, I receive more validation and the mind does not second guess the connection as much. This is also where some of my most amazing insights and creative ideas come from.

Dreams

It is not uncommon for our loved ones to appear to us in our dreams, and I have had a few such dreams since Blaine has transitioned. The most vivid one was of us riding in an older turquoise car. Perhaps it was his favorite; I am not sure. I was sitting in the front seat with him, he had his arm around me, and I had my head on his shoulder. In front of me was the most beautiful rainbow I have ever seen and ever will see. The colors were nothing like I ever could have imagined. I felt loved, held, and at peace. I have often wondered if I visit him in spirit at night in my dreams. Many spiritual coaches recommend keeping a journal by the bed to write down dreams. It is said that you can also ask your guides or angels to send you dreams about your loved one.

I had other dreams where Blaine and I were together in different ways. Some were nice; some not so much. In a podcast interview I did with Dr. Joshua Black, we discussed the fascinating research that he is doing as the Bereavement Initiative Manager for the BC Centre for Palliative Care. Dr. Black is one of the leading academic experts in "grief dreams," which can be dreams of the deceased. In his research, he found that through our dreams we are likely processing something from our waking life. He shared information on the importance of dreams in helping to process your emotions, the benefit of rescripting dreams, the value of dreams in understanding our grieving process, and we even discussed tips for getting a good night's sleep. He also has a fascinating story about how he got into the work that he does.[16]

If you have not experienced a grief dream, do not worry. It does not mean anything is wrong. You may be having dreams and not remembering them, or you might be processing in a different way. We are all different in the way we process our grief. If you are having troubling recurring dreams, it might be a good idea to find someone who can help you work through your experiences and give you strategies to deal with them.

Journal Exercises:

- What signs and guidance have you received? What kinds of symbols and signs would you like to receive?
- Imagine you have the power to grant wishes. Write about three wishes you would grant for yourself and three wishes you would grant for others.
- Write a letter to your future self, describing the life you envision for yourself and the goals you want to achieve in honor of your loved one.

Calls to Action:

- Find a special place to keep the things your loved one has left you such as feathers, dimes, or other treasures. Write down experiences you have that tell you your loved one is near. It can be comforting to go back and read these from time to time. I was always surprised at the ones I had forgotten. You may be surprised as you draw your attention to these messages how much more often you notice the signs.
- Check out the *Awaken Your Soul's Journey: Embracing Grief as a Pathway to Transformation* Podcast Episode 6: "Grief Dreams with Dr. Joshua Black" (see URL in Bibliography).

PART IV

Purpose and Expansion

Chapter 11

Awakening and Transformation

Stepping into the Unknown

I am now ready to step into my future with Blaine tucked safely in my heart. I am curious and filled with excitement to find out what is next. I am also scared, but the call to step forward and discover the unknown is strong.

Many people knew me as Blaine's wife, and I am honored to carry that experience and love and those cherished memories forward as I build my new life as Angela. Now Blaine guides me and cheers me on from his higher perspective, and I do my utmost to live life to the fullest. I am stepping into my purpose and making him proud. Blaine and I are doing this together.

Each time I go back to my hometown of Val Marie, memories come flooding in. I remember traveling with Blaine on Highway 4 to Swift Current for supplies, machinery parts, or hockey practice. We loved spending time together, and we had the greatest conversations as he drove. Each time I go to Val Marie, I feel gratitude and appreciation for all that we lived through in our thirty-five years of marriage. When I look back, I can see all that it was, all it meant, and how beautiful our life together was. The future, however, does not look so clear. Moving through grief is like driving through fog. We can barely see the road ahead, yet we trust that as we drive, the road will present itself. We keep moving because, deep down, we know the future will unfold. When we lose a loved one, it is up to us to shine our own light in the fog, find our way, step into the unknown, and surrender. Life goes on. There is more life to be lived—or we would not still be here.

There are creations waiting for us to give birth to them. Everyone has their own contribution to make in this world. What is behind us is no longer a viable option, and embracing the present moment and dreaming about the future helps us to move forward. There is a delicate balance between relishing the past and its beautiful memories and feeling into the excitement and joy the future can bring.

Sometimes when driving through fog, we see familiar things that help us find our way—a distinctive tree, a curve in the road, or a neighbor's yard light helps us get our bearings. In navigating grief, we might get our bearings by having coffee with a trusted friend, going for a walk, cuddling a pet, listening to our favorite music, or drinking a warm cup of tea. Sometimes we just need to call in support from someone up the road who can reach out and help us find our way. We can seek out a mentor, a therapist, a healer, or a coach who can keep us informed and grounded as we move through challenges. Finding a person with whom we resonate is important. That person can help ease our mind and provide a space in which we can become more curious about our journey. They can help us let go of the thoughts and beliefs clouding our perceptions and blocking our way and lift the fog so we can see the road ahead.

You do not need to rush through the fog. Keep a slow, steady pace. Each of us has a path in life. Each of us came to this earth with a life to live. There is a reason and a season for each of our challenges. One day, you will realize you have traveled far on your journey. Keep moving forward at your own pace, trusting as you go that the road will unfold in front of you exactly as it should. You cannot do it wrong. You are doing it your way!

Facing Fears

Driving down a foggy road can be scary. Sometimes we pull over and stop because we feel safer where we are. We are not happy, but we are afraid that what lies ahead might be worse. We become frozen, unable to move on. Educator and self-improvement leader Dan Charles Pope says that if you stay in the state of comfort, you are not growing. Sometimes it seems impossible for us to take that step. We are not happy where we are, but we cannot see ourselves in a place where we will be happy again. Sometimes we are not ready—and that is okay. Only you will know when it is time to take that step forward. When you face your fear and indecision and turn it into action, something powerful happens. Some people say that when you take one step toward healing, the universe takes ten for you.

Is there something you have been wanting to do? Some idea you have that you just cannot get out of your head? Are you missing out on opportunities because you are afraid to put yourself out there? Should you apply for that job? Take that class? Take that test? Do you think you need more practice, more instruction, more skill? After we lose someone we love, we might lose confidence. What we go through is hard. It shakes us up. Consider this: doing the things you have in mind will not be as bad as what you have gone through already. Going through hard things builds strength and resilience. You might be stronger than you think.

I have always had an underlying fear of putting myself in the spotlight and being heard. *What if I say something wrong?* In our administration meetings, I would have ideas, but I was afraid to voice them. *What if they seem silly?* I took courses for two Master of Education degrees online, one in Information Technology and the other in Distance Education. When I started my first online master's class, I was new to online learning. Discussion took place in a forum, and the class shared their understandings of the coursework. Participation was mandatory, and we were marked on our engagement. When I posted to the forum for the first time, I sat and looked at the submission button for a long time before I clicked it. I messaged my professor—I was ready to quit the program because putting my answer out there for everyone in the class to see was too much. The potential that someone might criticize my work was unbearable. He reassured me by explaining the online learning environment was new to me and it might take some getting used to and he would be there to help me through. Once I posted and realized that these were students and just like me were learning too, I felt better, and I completed the program. The same thing happened when I was about to submit my first blog post. I was terrified to publish it. Fortunately, I always had encouragement from others, and I got past my fear.

When I tell people I have these fears, they are surprised. Perhaps on the outside I look like I have got it together. Imagine a duck gliding on top of the water, but underneath, its feet are paddling like crazy—that was me. I was a school principal and had to speak at graduations and other events. I also performed at music festivals, recitals, weddings, and funerals. For each of those events, I was careful to have a script in front of me (or I practiced it so much I could recite it in my sleep). If I was not prepared, I jumbled and bumbled through, or I panicked and then beat myself up later for what I could have said or should have done. If someone pointed out a mistake, I was mortified! My mind kept replaying the event, and I kept beating myself up. Blaine helped me through those times. When I got home, he was always there. He encouraged me, talked things through with me, and reminded me he loved me. He gave me permission to believe in myself. Now that he is gone, it is up to me to reach out to others for support. Or, as I am discovering, I can support myself by recognizing when I am beating myself up and, if I make a mistake, I can show myself the compassion I deserve.

Despite my loss, I have taken on and overcome many challenges. I retired from my job. I do not live in the same community anymore. The familiar faces are gone. I knew if I did not put myself out there, it would get awfully lonely. It was terrifying. The first time I went curling in Maple Creek, I was happy to have the invite but I was nervous. I had not curled for years, and on top of it, there was not a soul there I knew. At one point, my anxiety was through the roof, and I thought I would have a stroke or a heart attack. I had to use

Blaine's stick because I could not bend down and throw the rock. It takes a fair bit of leg strength to get down on the ice and slide with the rock. Then you have to get back up! I tried the first couple of throws without the stick, but I knew I would need it for the rest of the game. *What would others think?* But I went back again, played with different teams, and met different people. It was hard, but I did it.

I also tried golfing in the summer. I liked the fact that I was getting out and exercising, and it was great for me to meet new people. I am not the greatest golfer. I really do not know where the ball will go when I hit it. Once in a while, I surprise myself by hitting a good drive. By the time I get to the ninth hole, I really just want to walk off and call it good. I do not understand people who can golf eighteen holes. I joined a lady's group. They are part of the Crown Jewels of Canada, and the chapter in Maple Creek is the Sassy Sapphires. I guess we are similar to those known as the Red Hatters. It is a support group for women. We wear cute headpieces or hats and the colors white and red or purple. Once a month we get together. A few of the women in the group also belong to the Superannuated Teachers group that I belong to here in town, so I see some familiar faces. The Superannuated Teachers meet and do things together, such as attend musicals, dine out in different places, and golf. I go when I feel like I can. Often, I am busy doing my own thing, so I am only taking in what feels right to me. Somehow, I am finding balance with it all.

I wanted to travel. Being on a plane for the first time without Blaine was sad. I was a couple months into this grief journey. Going through security made me nervous—those officials can be stern. I was compliant, but I was scared! The first time I went through that on my own, I thought I would faint. I could barely breathe. I was just sick about it ... but I did it, anyway. And you know what? I had an amazing trip and made beautiful memories.

The first time I was guided to hold an online summit for grief, I was filled with anxiety. I had sent invitations to people I did not know, and I was required to master technology I had never seen. I had never done interviews like this—I was interviewing experts in their fields, and their credentials intimidated me. But my guides sent me messages that I was on the right track and always guided and supported.

Recall that earlier I mentioned I received a message about "a conversation with Rita." I was not sure what it meant at the time, but I discovered later that it was spirit letting me know what I was going to do in the future. That there was indeed a plan. The first person who signed up to be interviewed for my first grief summit was named ... you guessed it ... Rita! I was learning to trust the messages I was getting. It was fun! All the people I met were amazing. Each time I met a new person, I could not believe how fortunate I was they would take the time to talk to me, tell me their story, and support my event. Once I completed the first ten interviews, I felt more comfortable. I learned so much from each of the speakers. The fear did not go away, but the joy of speaking to these people outweighed my anxiety, and I felt more confident. I put myself out there, in a bigger way, and trusted things would turn out. I felt the support of my guides, my angels, and certainly Blaine.

One of my psychic healers confirmed that Blaine had helped coordinate the summit for my benefit and that of my audience. He not only helped me find perfect people to bring through the information and resources I needed; he brought them in the perfect order for me to process my grief. My amazing mentor Adrien supported me the entire way too. I will always be grateful for what she, my guides, my angels, my ancestors, and many others did to help and encourage me.

Sometimes you do not know what you are capable of or what will bring you joy until you try. Each time I think about stepping into something new, I feel the fear, and I have learned to work through it. The fear does not go away—but you do not have to wait until you are comfortable or confident to do something you are called to do. You put yourself out there and follow what sparks your curiosity, excites you, and brings you joy.

One thing I have learned is that sometimes, something is not a problem until we make it one. For example, if I got an email from someone about things that were not working with the summit or I received feedback about mistakes I had made, I looked at it as a golden opportunity to chat with someone new. I did my best to make things right for them, and I met a lot of kind people through the process. Some of these people have become friends. I always wonder, *Were those mistakes made at the perfect time for a higher purpose?*

If there is any gift in this loss, it's that it's making me become my own, more independent person. I understand how strong I can be and that I will survive. I miss Blaine, yet his essence is here, guiding me, supporting me, cheering me on as I make each decision. When I mess up, I give myself a break. I can see him up there grinning and laughing with me, and loving me the way he did when he was here. I'm not perfect. Neither is anyone else. We're all human. There's no need to criticize ourselves when we're doing the best we can. No one can deny that this is a tough and sometimes lonely road. Not everything can work out perfectly. I must speak up for myself. I'm worth it, and I respect myself enough to call for respect from others in a loving way. I'm a work in progress. If I waited for a time that I felt like doing some of these things that I knew were going to be a little uncomfortable for me, I just wouldn't do them. What can you do today that is stepping a little out of your comfort zone? Allow yourself to stretch a little each day. You may be surprised at what you can achieve if you decide to take action.

Serving Others

I realized through presenting my summits, practicing my healing modalities, and writing my blog, I could help others. The summits were an opportunity to learn more about grief, to share what I had learned, and to help the speakers promote their work. It really was a triple win. The only thing that could have held me back was my fear. I knew if I held the right intentions going into each of these ventures, then my higher self would support and guide me each step of the way.

I held my first summit in June 2022. From there, I had a community of people on my email list who were looking for help. Grief and life coach Julie Cluff was holding a certification course starting that summer, so I signed up. I decided I would become a grief coach, and that would be a way I could offer support for those in my newly formed community.

In the fall, I held the first of what I call Grief Group Get-Togethers. I realized I could hold space on Zoom for anyone who would like to come. Through my intent, I could energetically provide a place for healing, acknowledgement, and support. In each meeting, the beautiful souls who joined shared their stories, and we had helpful discussions. Profound healing took place in that environment—both for those who attended and for me. I continue these sessions to this day. We have built a core group of amazing individuals who have so much wisdom and experience to bring. The group is going strong, and it fills my heart every time we meet. You can sign up to join the group.[17]

When I first started out with my new venture, I needed help. The people on my email list were like me when I lost Blaine. They were looking for information and suggestions and especially hope. It would become my mission to help others. *How could I help them? How should I proceed with my work?* As I noted earlier, I came to rely on advice from my guides. One way I connected with them was by setting up an altar and placing pictures and mementos of my ancestors on it. Many times, I sat in this special place and breathed through my fear. I asked my angels, my helpers, and Blaine for assistance. Sitting quietly, I waited for inspiration and answers. I talked to them, told them my thoughts, my feelings, and my issues. Each time I took a step toward creating my dream, I got more confident.

Since starting my summits, others have interviewed me on their podcasts and online forums. I look forward to these interviews. I enjoy the opportunity to tell my story, and even if only one person benefits from one thing I share, I am overjoyed. I still get nervous, of course. But I speak honestly and openly, have fun, enjoy the experiences, and feel grateful for the opportunities. Sharing my story in the blog posts can also make me a little anxious. I try not to worry about what others might think or that I will make mistakes. In the end, my intention is to be of help. Helping others, by sharing my story and what I have learned, gives me purpose and meaning.

Is there something you want to do that will bring you joy and support others? I hope this will inspire you to take the next step. Anything that brings you joy can also be a beautiful gift to help someone else. Take one small step. Ask for help and inspiration. Face the fear and do it, anyway. You will be glad you did. I believe in you!

Exercises:

- Recognize what kinds of experiences and opportunities you might want to explore. What fears are holding you back?

Identify Fear (e.g., Being alone, making connections, facing financial challenges.)	Challenge Fear (Are these realistic, or are they rooted in anxiety or self-doubt?)	Break Down Fear (e.g., Reach out for support, join a community, attend classes.)	Set Small Goals (e.g., Attend one social event per month.)	Action (Growth happens outside your comfort zone. What small step can you take?)

- An altar or any designated space for ritual can be a wonderful way to honor a loved one. Here are some suggestions for how to set this up:
  1. Choose a space in your home or outdoors. It could be a table, a shelf, a windowsill, or a place outside under a tree or in your garden. I simply have a shelf.
  2. Collect items that hold significance. Examples: candles, flowers, personal belongings, or other objects that represent your loved one's hobbies or interests. I have some stones, little ornaments, and pictures. My grandma collected little mice figurines, so I have a little ceramic ornament of mice. Purple reminds me of my aunt, so I have an amethyst stone. I have pictures and a candle to honor Blaine. Anything goes.

3. Arrange the items any way you'd like. You can create different levels by adding books or boxes. I have them arranged all on one level.

4. Incorporate elements of nature. I have some special stones I picked up, some seeds, and some feathers.

5. Light candles. They could be flameless candles. I often light the candle when I sit at the altar.

6. Light incense or add flowers to create a beautiful scent around your altar.

7. Incorporate some kind of ritual or practice. Sometimes I meditate there, or I journal or pray. Sometimes I play my drum or just have a conversation. On occasion, I take a Kit Kat bar (Blaine loved those) and eat it while I talk. I have even offered up a piece to share while I am sitting there with my ancestors.

8. You can refresh and update your altar as time goes on. Treat it as a sacred space, and visit it regularly. There is no right or wrong way to do this. Trust your instincts. Do what is meaningful to you.

Chapter 12

Understanding Self

The Complexity of Being Human

Many of us dream about our retirement, being free from the obligations of work and free to do whatever we want whenever we want. I imagined this time too. I planned to tackle all the projects I had been longing to do: start up some creative adventure, travel, read, learn a new skill. Well, here I am in that place I dreamed I would be someday. I am, in fact, retired. Acquiring an in-depth knowledge of grief was not something I expected to be doing. Still, I find the work interesting and rewarding, and I enjoy learning more about what I am going through so I can help myself and others.

If I said I did not feel angry sometimes about this space I have found myself in, I would be lying. There is a human aspect of me that asks, *Why did my soul choose this experience?* Sometimes she needs to be acknowledged. I have learned to "put my arm around her," so to speak, and acknowledge her frustration with her soul's choices. I have learned we human beings live multidimensional lives. That common saying, "there is a part of me ..." is one I never understood until lately.

Once, my coach Julie Cluff and I were having a session, and she pulled out three emotion cards. These cards work much like angel cards. They were designed by energy and life coach Julie Hawkes. Each card has an action and a journal prompt to help you explore and process your emotions. The cards for that day were hatred, discouragement, and blame. I was shocked. *Why did a dark set of emotion cards come up?* I was in the middle of my fourth series of the summit and writing this book. *What do I have to hate? Why would I be discouraged? Who is to blame?*

I saw that just because part of me is enjoying what I am doing on a day-to-day basis, does not mean there are not other parts of me that are still wounded. When our emotions feel the opportunity is right for healing, they will show themselves. As Julie and I felt into the energy, we discovered a part of me that hated that this was the life I chose. I hated that Blaine was gone. I was discouraged about how difficult this road can be, and that piece of me wanted to blame Blaine, God, or myself for putting me in this situation. I know this human part of me wants to be acknowledged—and rightfully so. I cannot keep shushing her each time she comes up to be heard. I started to understand the complexity of the healing process. I had been ignoring that little voice.

A few people have asked me, "Are you enjoying retirement?" "Do you miss your job?" These are hard questions to answer. Retirement looks nothing like I thought it would because I had planned it to be Blaine and me together. *What will my retirement look like without him?* Each time I do something on my own, I am building a bridge to freedom. It is awkward and hard sometimes yet also auspicious. As I step into something new and feel empowered, I may still have to deal with a part of myself that is afraid or disappointed about how my retirement has played out. I acknowledge that part of me, and with love and kindness, I bring her along on this adventure she did not ask for. The more I acknowledge and support her, the easier she can accept this part of the journey. It is up to me to recognize this, and I must be accountable for my healing. It is in my best interest to take responsibility for all the parts of me.

Mary Sise, a leading voice in the advancing field of energy psychology, pioneered a method she calls the soul-weaving process. She uses this as part of her practice along with EFT or "tapping." In our interview, she asked me to go back to a place that was traumatic for me. I chose the moment Blaine died. She helped me tap through that experience, and then, through her soul-weaving process, she led me back to that time and place. She guided me to put my arm around that part of myself and to let that "me" know, "I'm okay now. I'm helping others and learning to live this new life." It was a profound healing experience, and it taught me there is so much more to us than what we think there is. It helped me comprehend the complexity of our human selves. I understand better how love and compassion are the keys to healing all our wounded parts. Recognizing that emotions can often coexist or overlap can help us know ourselves better.

Life Number Two

As I reflect on my grief, it is hard to believe how much has transpired since Blaine passed to spirit. It feels like I am living another life. As Shawn Doyle suggested, I might call it Life Number Two. Stepping into this life, I have the freedom to choose. What do I want it to be? I realized I could live a happy life again. Not the same as it was, of course, because that is not possible anymore. Yet, as sad as that is, I have an opportunity to start out brand new. I needed to reinvent myself. I did not know what that might look like, but I could not see myself sitting at home being sad for the rest of my life either. Even with the pain, deep down I knew I had to find my joy and live it. It is possible for you too.

My second life has begun. Every day, I make my way into this new life, embrace my future, live each day as it comes, and get more comfortable with Life Number Two. I will always look back fondly on Life Number One with such gratitude and love. I will never, ever forget it. How could I forget something so amazing? Blaine loved me and truly only ever wanted me to be happy. Love never dies. So, I will look forward with gratitude, excitement, and hope as I step into my new life in the unknown. After living Life Number One with my husband and best friend, I know exactly how great a life well lived can be! Blaine showed me how to live life to the fullest every day, and I plan to take his lead and live a Life Number Two that will make him proud.

I do not pretend to know your life or your circumstances. Maybe you are older or younger than me. Maybe you have financial difficulties. Maybe you have no family and are alone. Everyone's situation is different. However, like I said earlier, I do not believe you would still be here if you did not have work to do. All the challenges in the world cannot stop your inner drive to fulfill your purpose. It is your light, and if you allow it to, it will guide you through all of your challenges. I believe you have a Life Number Two in you. You just might not know yet what that looks like for you.

It is okay to step into Life Number Two not knowing what is next. In fact, that is the only way you step into it. As I mentioned earlier, one of the most difficult things is not knowing the answer to the question, "What is next?" If someone had told me I would be holding online summits and interviewing grief experts, I would have had a hard time believing it. Had someone told me I would be putting myself out there, I would have said, "No way." It would have been overwhelming. It is best to concentrate on one thing at a time. Thinking about the final product can create anxiety, worry, and fear. We do not need to know how it will turn out, but we do need to take a step, try things, and make mistakes along the way. My Grandma Grace used to use the phrase "little by little." She was wise. You only need to take one little step to get started down the path to building your new life.

You are probably saying, "Well, Angela, I do not even know what to do first." I thought that way too. There were many times I did not know what I was doing or what to do next. Look at things this way—if we do not know who we are or what we are doing, that means anything is possible! We are starting fresh, with a clean slate of possibilities. Why waste it? I could not always visualize what I wanted, yet I knew how I wanted to *feel* in my new life. I wanted to live a life that felt fulfilled. I did not know how that could happen, but I hoped I would get there. I trusted that if I wanted it and allowed it, it would come—and it did.

I believe the universe, or our higher self, sends us clues to what our next step will be. Most of the time we focus on things we need to do and think so much about the past or the future that we forget we are living a life right now in this moment. When we are thinking and doing, we ignore all the signs and messages all around us. We "fall asleep," so to speak. We get used to living this way. Soon, we do what we have always done, or we do what someone tells us to do. Without thinking things through, days, weeks, and years can go by—and this is what I am trying to avoid. I want to live mindfully and authentically. Breaking the habit of mindless doing is challenging. It takes diligence and practice.

About a year into my healing, I was looking at Christmas cards and saw one from Blaine that said, "to my wifey." I miss being Blaine's "wifey." I miss having someone suggest to me what to do next. It is funny, I never liked having anyone, including Blaine, tell me what to do, yet now I wish I could get it back. Sometimes, I get tired of self-monitoring. If I do not do the dishes or do the laundry, or if I eat an entire bag of chips and three chocolate bars, no one would know. I do not even know if anyone would care until it got so out of hand that it required intervention. (Good luck stopping me! I have eaten so much chocolate, I could turn into a cocoa bean!) The only person keeping that in check is me. I no longer have a superintendent to tell me what I should focus on or a group of parents or children who have expectations of me. That should be a relief. It should be freeing. Instead, it seems like a lot of responsibility.

I am fortunate. There are people who help and support me. However, if I cannot count on myself to take initiative, be accountable, stand up, and realize what I need for myself, there are going to be problems. We have to step into the space where we start looking after ourselves. We have been making decisions in consideration of others for so long, we do not know what we want. A member of my Grief Get-Together Group mentioned she realized she could change her space. She changed her flooring. She equated it with laying a new foundation in her life. I thought she expressed that beautifully. Take time to sit still. Reflect. Then take some little steps. Try some new things. They do not have to be big things or even expensive things, just things that bring you joy.

I am the one who decides to be miserable or happy. I decide what my house looks like, what I do, what I eat, what I say, whom I meet ... all of it. This may feel like a lot when we are trying to survive our grief, but it is important. Our mind can make up many reasons not to follow our joy. It feels hard. It takes too much time. We are busy or not capable. Each time you accomplish some small task, relish in the fact. Say, "I did it!" Celebrate your step forward!

I am learning that life does not have to be overwhelming or hard unless I judge it so. No matter where we are in our grief journey, it is a good time to take a hard look at how we show up for ourselves. You have to make it all about you now because if you do not, you will not be able to be there for anyone else. What are your values? Your goals? What are you doing to move toward those goals? How can you experience joy every day as you work toward those goals? How can you make sure you do not forget to enjoy every moment in the process?

Authenticity and the True Self

I aim to discover who I am now without Blaine. I want to know what it means to be authentic. I want to be real, genuine, and sincere and act in accordance with my own beliefs and values. My values serve as my moral compass, and that makes it easier for me to make choices and plan action.

What is meaningful to you? Knowing your values is critically important for knowing yourself. If you want to be yourself and stand up for yourself, you need to ask, "What am I standing up for?" Knowing what you will and will not tolerate allows you to set boundaries without feeling guilty or pressured.

Blaine helped me set my boundaries. He pointed out when I was working too much and he helped me sort out conflicts with others. Sometimes, when I allowed others to take advantage of who I was, he let me know it. I admired Blaine for that, and I admire others who know what they stand for and can say what they believe without fear or shame.

I always thought setting boundaries had to result in conflict. I was never one for conflict or a hard conversation, and I think that is true for many of us. I avoided difficult conversations if I could. Looking back, I realize that if I had been clear on my values, I may have found it easier to speak up. If we discuss perspectives openly, we can approach conflict with empathy and find a solution that reflects our key values. Being open-hearted and aligning with my values helps me speak freely. I respond to conflict with love for myself and who I am, rather than becoming defensive or giving in to outside pressure.

We will know when we are not upholding our values because we will have a sense of inner conflict or dissatisfaction. When we experience guilt, shame, or dissonance, it is a sign we are not connected with our inner truth. For example, as a teacher and principal, I spent extra time at work because of all the demands of running a school. I had a strong desire to do a good job for the students and the community. If you know anything about the education profession, you know teachers and administrators could work twenty-four hours a day and never get everything done. I always made a point of attending family events, but often a good part of my weekends and evenings were taken up with marking or planning. Looking back, I was always in conflict, trying to balance my time and my values. I was spending quality time with my family while upholding the demands of doing more to create opportunities for the students at my school. Often, I felt imbalanced. Blaine was incredibly patient and supportive through it all. It is one of many things I dearly miss about him.

A search online using the words, "How will I know my values?" produces quizzes and simple lists that will help you define your values. At the end of this chapter, I will provide some suggestions for determining your own values and how they can help guide you in your life going forward.

Self-Love

Self-love is crucial because it provides a foundation for healing and helps build resiliency. As I noted earlier, grief brings about a range of emotions. Experiencing sadness, anger, and guilt along with other powerful emotions can be overwhelming. The approach to any of these feelings is self-compassion, treating yourself with kindness and understanding. If we can get this kind of support from others, that is wonderful. But the truth is, often we need to comfort and support ourselves. We need to make self-compassion a priority and not judge ourselves, nor react to others' judgment. Sometimes it is hard to get past the things we do not like about ourselves to bring compassion and love to all of who we are, but it is essential that we do so.

Self-love is also a way to honor the memory of our loved one. By taking care of yourself and living a life that aligns with your values, you honor your loved one's memory. Continuing your own personal growth and pursuing your passions is what your loved one would want for you.

I cannot stress enough that going through the grieving process can be draining physically. Getting rest, eating well, exercising, and finding support is essential. We need to prioritize our needs and take care of ourselves. No one knows better than we do what we truly need. In the beginning stages of grief, self-care can be difficult. Often, we are accustomed to putting others before ourselves because we were taught it was the "right" thing to do. If looking after ourselves is contradictory to our belief systems, we resist. Sometimes we busy ourselves to keep from feeling. But we cannot be of value or service to anyone without looking after ourselves first. We cannot pour anything from an empty cup. It is that simple. Filling the cup up starts with taking time to feel into your body and ask, "What do I need?"

Exercises:

- Take the time to find out what your values are. Brené Brown suggests you start with just two.[18] Choose two and write them somewhere—perhaps on a sticky note on your fridge or by your desk at work. Write down a detailed description of what a life with these values looks like, including the actions, behaviors, and relationships that reflect the values you have chosen. Write down some decisions that you are contemplating now or will have to address in the future. Ask yourself, "Which choice is most in line with what I believe and value?" This can help guide you toward decisions that are true to your authentic self.

- Set an alarm on your phone to alert you every couple of hours to check in with yourself. Stop, be still, and determine what your body might need. How are you feeling? Where is it tight? Are there sore parts? What are you thinking about? Your body is clear when it is thirsty, hungry, or tired. But it will also let you know when you might need quiet reflection or more interaction with others. If you make it a priority to pay attention to your body and provide what it needs, it will respond favorably.
- Create a Character Board: This board can be as elaborate or as simple as you'd like. Put your name (in bold letters) and your picture (optional) on a piece of paper or posterboard. Fill the board with words and/or pictures that describe how you want to feel, what character traits you want to embody, and what kind of person you want to be. Here are some examples of words you might include on your board:
  - beautiful
  - calm
  - connected
  - courageous
  - curious
  - fearless
  - free
  - grateful
  - honest
  - inspiring
  - intuitive
  - kind
  - loving
  - loyal
  - peaceful

- playful
- strong
- sweet
- truthful
- wise

- Then, each day, look at your board and add the words "I am" before each of your words. Read the phrases out loud: "I am kind," "I am fearless," "I am curious," etc. You can add things you want to be as well, such as "writer," "leader," "speaker," or "humanitarian." Then you can say "I am a writer," "I am a speaker," and so on.
- Hang your character board up where you can see it every day. Make the statements out loud as often as you can.

Chapter 13

Acceptance and Self-Forgiveness

Acceptance and Surrender

Some things are simply out of our control. For example, I am not a big fan of windy days. I cannot change the fact that the wind is blowing, so how does judging a windy day help me? I am learning that I have the ability to change my thoughts about the wind ... or at least stop judging it. I believe this concept applies to all things over which we have no control.

I recall "The Serenity Prayer":

God, grant me the serenity to accept the things I cannot change,
the courage to change the things I can,
and the wisdom to know the difference.[19]

This prayer was on our wall in our house when I was growing up. I remember looking at it and wondering, *What does it mean?* Now, through my loss, I understand. Sometimes we recognize that things just are what they are. They cannot be changed. Then we need to turn inward and decide, *What am I going to do about it?* Sometimes, we take small steps to change our thoughts, which in turn change our emotions. I do my best to trust there is a purpose for everything, even if I do not understand it. Even the wind!

A friend sent me some information she learned in one of her psychology classes. It was about The Wheel of Life, a medieval model of change. I found it interesting. There are four emotions on this wheel: happiness, loss, suffering, and hope. In this paradigm, we move through life starting from happiness at the top of the wheel, at the 12:00 position. We move to the position of loss at 3:00, then to suffering at 6:00. Finally, we move to hope at 9:00 and back to happiness again. When loss happens in life (and it will), we want to get back to happiness as fast as we can, so we try to go backward on the wheel. It does not work that way. We must move in a clockwise direction, because the only way back to happiness is through suffering and hope. Suffering is the phase on the wheel of life that represents transition. The Latin word for suffering is *sufferre*, "to experience or allow." We cannot go around that which causes us to suffer. We must go through it. Out of suffering, hope arises. Suffering involves unpleasant feelings: tension, stress, anxiety, worry, frustration, anger, conflict. When we surrender to those unpleasant feelings, we can move forward.

Facing the loss, pain, and suffering of losing Blaine was the only way for me to get back to hope. In my darkest hours, I realized that without hope, there was no way back to happiness. Just like there is no way to stop the wind—we can only move through it—I am here to tell you that beyond your suffering and pain there is hope. There is happiness again. Have faith. Trust. Surrender to the process.

The wind does not blow every day, and when it does, I know there will be a new day. Everything changes. In the meantime, I need to find ways to have compassion for my human self, who struggles with sad days of grief. I need to take time to do something I love to do. Maybe I bake my favorite treat, mix up Grandma's stew recipe and slow cook it in my Crock-Pot, or treat myself to a warm bath or a massage. Maybe I stay in my pajamas, read my favorite book, or watch my favorite show. I do whatever I can for myself to make my day better. I give myself love. I surrender to what is, tell myself it is okay to be miserable, but also realize I can change my thoughts. I am in control, and I can choose not to judge those windy or sad days. I can let them be what they are. Windy. Sad. This too shall pass—if we surrender.

As I learned to work through my emotions and let go, I started feeling better. Little by little, I found joy. This gave me hope for the future. Self-love and understanding are key to healing from grief. It is opening your heart to love yourself. To love life again. I looked at myself with compassion and appreciation for how I was taking time for myself, making choices for my benefit. Having patience and gratitude for my unique journey made me available to be there for others. It became a win-win situation.

Releasing emotion is exhausting work, so sleep is imperative. Hot baths, healing meditations, and daily energy routines were an important part of my routine for months. Invest in your future. Take small steps toward healing in as many ways as you can. You are not going to feel better immediately. Over time, these things pay off. I took long walks in nature, and sometimes I could feel my heart opening. The warm sun on my face, the sound of water running in the creek, and the familiar smells of the season comforted me. I played music as I walked. Sometimes '90s dance tunes, sometimes a walking meditation, or soft, healing music like that of Paul Luftenegger. I thought about how trees love to recycle, and I sent my sadness to them, imagining they would transform it into pure, clean air for the planet. I hugged the big pine tree in my yard just because I could. The plants in my house became a solace for me. I gathered rocks and crystals and learned about their properties and how they could be powerful healing agents. I studied essential oils and used them as appropriate. I started to understand how Mother Earth has provided so much to help us heal.

Blaine and I used to take walks together from our ranch down Hillandale Road. The fresh air, the smell of sage, and the softness of the rolling hills were all holding us as we talked about the problems we had faced that day. Often, by the time we returned home, we felt lighter, freer, and able to tackle whatever was ahead of us. Now, looking back, I could see that Mother Nature had been taking care of us even when we did not recognize it. I remember stepping outside in the morning, listening to the chattering creek that ran through our yard. It was so powerful and captivating. I stood and listened to it before rushing off to work. Now I find solace in the sound of running water. I imagine my emotions being carried away, and the water healing my soul. My heart is opening and healing. I am opening to my future.

Forgiving as an Act of Self-Love

Accepting and forgiving ourselves is part of the healing process for grief. It is said that life is for giving, and forgiveness is the ultimate act of generosity. Accepting ourselves as imperfect and forgiving ourselves for any perceived shortcomings or unresolved matters is self-love. If we allow ourselves to let go of self-blame and focus on healing, we can move forward. It is so easy to blame ourselves for things left unsaid, things not done, or for disagreements we may have had with a loved one. It is not so easy to forgive. In the end, in any situation, we are all doing the best we can.

Forgiving others for perceived wrongdoings is another tough part of the grieving process. For example, I was so angry at the oncologist for not following up with me after Blaine passed. We had talked to him on the phone about once a month for ten months. He would go over Blaine's plan and answer our questions. On our last phone call, I could tell it was difficult for the oncologist. He said something like, "I hate this stupid disease." I could hear the emotion in his voice. When Blaine transitioned, I never heard from the man who, until Blaine died, I felt had been an intimate part of our lives. I thought he might send a letter or a message. Nothing. It bothered me. When we put our beloved dog and cat to rest, we got a card signed by the entire vet's office expressing their sympathies for our loss. It was thoughtful. We did not know them that well, but I really appreciated that they reached out. I considered sending the oncologist's office assistant a set of cards for him to have signed and ready so she could just send one out each time they lost a patient. That might sound ridiculous, but I had mixed feelings—I was hurt and angry that he had not followed up, yet at the same time, I felt empathy and compassion for everything this doctor had to deal with in his practice. I know

I will never understand how difficult it must be to deal with this disease day in and day out. I saw enough of it in those ten months to know I did not want to hold on to this. So, I forgave him. I believe that he could have followed up, but I am accepting that it did not happen because he was just too busy. Not because he did not care. I have also learned a valuable lesson about the importance of small gestures, such as an acknowledgement in grief.

If we are the victim of a horrific trauma, such as homicide or abuse, forgiveness might feel like we are dismissing what happened. Showing empathy and compassion does not give anyone a pass for having abused someone else, nor for the consequences of that abuse. If we have been hurt, it is likely we have built up a wall of pain, and we will need guidance and support to break it down and let go of resentment. Perhaps in time, we can let that person go, knowing they must find their own way on their own healing journey. Forgiveness, in fact, is a gift we give to ourselves. Forgiving is a way of releasing our resentment and pain.

Spiritual teacher Dr. Joe Vitale brought the ancient Hawaiian forgiveness practice of Ho'oponopono into the modern spiritual movement. Ho'oponopono is a powerful and remarkable spiritual and healing practice. The prayer is, "I'm sorry. Please forgive me. Thank you. I love you." Ho'oponopono is often used as a form of self-reflection and healing, aiming to release negative emotions and promote inner peace. You can find a quiet space, take some deep breaths, and repeat these four key phrases, imagining sending these words and intentions toward a particular person or situation. Repeat the phrases as many times as you feel necessary, letting the process fill you up with gratitude and love.

Julie Cluff had me create a Ho'oponopono chart containing a list of memories. I categorized the list into four vertical columns. The first column was titled "I am sorry for," then "I forgive you for," then "I thank you for," and then, "I love you for." Once I listed my memories in each of those columns, I wrote a letter to Blaine using that list. The letter was profoundly healing for me, and the process of reading it out loud to my coach was even more cathartic.

I have included the initial letter I wrote as an example. The intent is to do the exercise, not to comment on it or to analyze it. The letter below is a snapshot of my thoughts at that time and was an opportunity for me to release what was on my mind. If I wrote it again today, it would look different. What is in the letter is not important. What was important was the process of writing it and reading it aloud. If you try this exercise, I recommend you go through the process slowly, in small bites, with good support. It can bring up very tender emotions.

Dear Blainie,

There are a few things I thought I would share with you now that you are on the other side. Perhaps some of this you know already, but I am sure you would like to hear it again, and it helps me to process all I am thinking and feeling when I write, so here goes.

First of all, I am sorry you had to suffer through all you had to with cancer. I wish there had been better methods for healing than chemotherapy, and I wish we could have found someone that could have helped you more, or I could have somehow helped you more. I am sorry you had so much stress to deal with financially and otherwise with the ranch. You always remained positive, and yet it seemed those issues were relentless. I am sorry you and I didn't get to spend our retirement together, and sorry you hardly had any time to enjoy yours. I am sorry we didn't get that trip across Canada together in the motorhome you talked about, and you didn't get your Mustang. I am sorry I didn't take the time or feel the urgency to support you a little more with those goals and others you wanted to achieve, like getting your Class 1 license. I am sorry you didn't get to be a grandpa here on earth and you could not walk your daughter down the aisle. I am sorry we could not spend our last Christmas together as a family and we could not grow old together.

I forgive you for all the times you pushed my buttons and got my goat. I forgive you for the times you got impatient and lost your temper. I forgive you for leaving first and leaving me here all alone in this house.

I thank you for proposing when you did and loving me fully and completely with unwavering devotion for 35 years. I thank you for letting me stand alongside you as a rancher's wife. I thank you for being a dad to our two amazing children. We did a great job of raising them together. I thank you for your love of sports and passion for hockey. I thank you for coaching those young curlers and making an impact in their lives. I thank you for accompanying, chaperoning, and being official chauffeur for my school field trips and for all the support you gave me throughout my career by attending all the Christmas concerts, music recitals, talent shows, and any other events I was a part of. I thank you for our vacations together, our camping trips to Cypress every summer, and our weekends at the spa in Moose Jaw. I thank you for our many walks together where we solved all our problems. Thank you for being such a great host and loving to entertain friends and family. It was truly a gift of yours to entertain people.

Thank you for saying, "I love you," and telling me I am beautiful every single day—sometimes several times. Thank you for encouraging me to follow my dreams, helping me to build my confidence, and always having my back.

I love your sense of humor and the way you can always make people laugh. I love your determination to be heard and your ability to connect with anyone and to say what you think with no hesitation. I love your bravery and courage for facing cancer and your positive attitude. I love you for your funny ways of saying things like, "Let's go to Tim Hornets" when you wanted a Tim Horton's coffee or "I am going to Peavey Mark" when you were off to buy ranch supplies at Peavey Mart. I love you for helping us find our seasonal site in Cypress and this beautiful home. I love you for continuing to be so close, for loving me and supporting me from heaven, and for being a big part of making me who I am today. I love that we get to continue our relationship in spirit. I know you are always there for me.

Your best friend always and in all ways,

Love, Angela

This exercise was freeing, comforting, and honoring for me. As time went on, I thought of things to add to the lists. Just because we forgive ourselves or someone else does not mean we cannot continue to express our pain. We can acknowledge our pain and choose to forgive. We can establish boundaries, hold people accountable, and let go of the hurt that came with their actions.

There is no rush to forgive. We can take as much time as we need. Forgiveness comes as we do the work of healing.

Standing on Your Own Two Feet

When I lost Blaine, I lost my support system, my safety net, my comfort. I had come home every day knowing he would be there for me. I know I am one of the lucky ones. He would have done anything and everything for me.

I had to learn to stand on my own, and I did not like it. At first, it felt way too hard. Everything I went to do became one big catalyst for pain. Yet somewhere in the depths of my soul, I converted all his support over all those years into a sense of confidence. It felt like there was a light inside my heart. Even though my mind was saying, "You can't do this," a little voice in my heart was saying, "Oh yes, you can!"

The spring following Blaine's passing, I went to our seasonal spot in Cypress Hills Provincial Park and opened the camper. I had been eager to get to our site. We acquired this campsite in 2019 after Blaine put our names on a waiting list with the owners who were building it. In the summer of 2017, he had moved our previous camper eight times to make sure I had a full summer of camping. It is challenging to book a spot for long length of time because of the demand. In the regular camping areas, you have to get on the internet on a certain day and time to get into an electronic queue. You would be really fortunate to get a site for six weeks. Now, with the seasonal spot, I can make a lease payment each year and leave the camper in this site year-round. Each winter, it has to be drained and winterized. This means putting antifreeze in all the lines and making sure chairs, tables, and other items are put away for the winter months.

I find Cypress Hills Park to be the most healing place in the world for me. The trees call to me like long-lost friends. They welcome me as I am. Since I was a young child, I have been going to what we just always called "the park." We went as a family often, and after Blaine and I were married, I spent practically every summer holiday soaking up the beauty in those trees. Back then, we would haul the camper up to the park and set up camp in one of the regular sites. It was the way I recharged after a long school year. I longed for the day I could get to the park, let my stress go, and relax. It is what got me through some busy years as an educator.

I had never set up the camper without Blaine. He was the one to hook up the power, water, and sewer. I always helped, yet I never had to worry about knowing a bunch about it all because we did it together. It was his thing. My thing was getting the inside of the camper ready and putting the slides out. It was (for the most part) an easy job. There is a button inside that you push to make the slides come out. It made so much more room in the camper to have the slide-outs. Blaine would let me know when we were ready to do that. It is funny. When you are married for thirty-five years, you each have your jobs. You know what the other person is thinking, and there is comfort in having those roles down so well. It is automatic.

On the twenty-minute drive from my home in Maple Creek out to the park, I felt sadness welling up. I felt cheated. *He should be here beside me. How much fun would this be if he were here?* I imagined both of us retired, excited to enjoy another season of camping together. But that was gone too. I learned to keep Kleenexes everywhere, including in the car. By this time, I had gotten used to things being this way, and I surrendered to the process. Out of each of my crying sessions came healing—and another good blog post.

What I felt once I arrived in the park is hard to explain. I was happy to be in the trees, and a sense of peace fell over me. Everything was familiar, yet nothing was the same. I was alone. My mind was trying to adjust to Blaine not being there physically. There was no excitement or relief about school being done for the year. More than anything, I missed Blaine's excitement. He, too, loved coming to the park, and he knew how important it was to me. He knew what I needed, and he never thought twice about it. Sometimes I think he knew me better than I knew myself.

I realized if I was going to stand on my own two feet, I would need to figure out how to provide myself with support and comfort. I spent that summer adjusting to being at the park alone. That meant going out to the park for short stays. It was difficult, so I spent only a couple nights at a time. In between visits, I would go back home to Maple Creek and help Sheldon and Whitney with their wedding planning. When I was at the park, I would allow myself to relax. I took long walks down the paths. I listened to music, and I breathed.

That fall, I winterized the camper all by myself. This meant draining the hot water heater and the sewer lines, putting antifreeze in all the lines, unhooking the sewer pipes and the electricity. I cleaned the inside of the camper and put in the slides. If a person does not winterize the camper correctly, all the lines will freeze and break. To avoid potential freezing, it all had to be done by September 20. It was a hard day because I was nervous about being able to do it by myself, and the emotional toll made it even more difficult. I was pretty angry that I was left to do this, but I was determined. I watched some YouTube videos, wrote some notes, and made it happen. I got through it. The pipes did not freeze, and this past summer (the second without Blaine) was better. I stayed in the park longer and enjoyed it. I started writing this book and did some reading and painting.

I am standing on my own two feet.
Sometimes my legs feel weak,
but I am standing and getting stronger every day.

Alone versus Lonely

One thing I am doing my best to learn is to be with myself and to enjoy spending time alone again. I used to love my alone time. When you are a wife and a mom and have a full-time job with extra things going on, there is never much alone time. I remember how I used to cherish a night or a day in the house by myself. I had shut off the television (it always seemed to be blaring), sat in the quiet, and thought about things I wanted to do with my free time—things I had been longing to have time to do. It felt good to daydream that way. Now I have all kinds of alone time, and I have to figure out what I want to do with it.

When you are grieving, sometimes you feel lonely. Suggestions and advice for combating loneliness include contacting friends or family, going out, joining a club, getting a pet, or finding a hobby. These suggestions are all helpful, to a point. At the end of the day, when you have to go home, you want your person. Also, being with others *and* feeling lonely is a thing. Sometimes, you do not feel like you are a part of the conversation. Sometimes you cannot relate. I have had that happen. I will be sitting with others in a coffee shop or at an event and they are talking about the drama in their lives. Maybe there is too much laundry or too much work. Maybe there has been a misunderstanding among family members or colleagues that is causing stress. I remember when my life was like that too. I could relate. Sometimes I feel like I would like to go back. I cannot. Everything has changed for me. It means that my priorities have changed, and therefore so have my relationships. It can be challenging and lonely at times.

In the beginning, when I returned home from a holiday—Vancouver, Arizona, Europe—I got sick. Most of the time, my stomach gave me trouble. Once it was COVID-19. I believe those illnesses were emotional effects of feeling lonely in my home. When I felt into the issue, the energy in the house felt what I can only describe as "sad." It makes sense. We moved to this house in Maple Creek in April 2021 after Blaine's diagnosis. All my memories in the house were of him being sick. Each time I came home, that energy closed in on me. I mentioned this to my coach, and she suggested I clear the house with intention. I focused in on each room and imagined it filled with love and light. I burned sage, and I ran it through each room. I put black crystals in each of the farthest four corners of the house. I redecorated the living room with a few new pieces. My cousin Holly helped me pick out suitable items. It was all very freeing.

The most profound energetic clearing happened out in my back yard. I was sitting and looking at the trees, thinking, *I feel like a stranger in my own home.* When I sit in silence, magical things happen. I heard this message in my mind, "Angela, this is your home. You are welcome here!" The message was accompanied by a sense of delight. I felt that all the nature that lived in my back yard was supporting me, surrounding my home and showering it with love and admiration. I love my home now. It is a work in progress as I reorganize it the way I want it, and it is comfortable and perfect for me. It is amazing how intention can shift the energy and make a big difference in our everyday lives.

After I had dealt with the energy in my home, and I felt better, I needed to deal with the loneliness. When you go from having someone with you every day to being by yourself, it is a big adjustment. Blaine and I were inseparable, and with him gone, some days were okay, some were not. I missed him most when I was hanging out with nothing pressing to do, when I was unwinding, or when I did not feel like starting a project or doing anything productive. There are always lots of things a person can do, but sometimes you do not feel like doing any of it. That is when I felt lonely. Feeling lonely is a normal part of grief. However, being alone does not have to feel lonely.

There are tools out there to help you through feelings of loneliness. You can get back to happiness and joy. There is pleasure, peace, love, and even excitement on the other side of grief. Please know: *It's possible.* I enjoy my alone time now. I am still working out what I want to do with my time, but I am feeling more confident every day.

Journal Questions:

- How did The Wheel of Life help you understand how you can move through the four primary emotions and return to happiness?
- When feelings rise up inside us, it feels like we need to do something about them, doesn't it? We don't. Sometimes we just need to be with those feelings and acknowledge they are there. That is where I have found relief. Try writing your thoughts of loneliness into your journal. See how acknowledging your feelings helps them to lose their intensity and opens you up to new solutions and possibilities.

Exercise:

- Letter Writing: After taking a few deep breaths and addressing a letter to your loved one, begin with a greeting. You may use the example from the chapter or just write whatever is on your mind at this time. There is no right or wrong way to do this.
- Then, read the letter out loud to yourself or someone you trust.

Chapter 14

Reconciliation and Finding Meaning

Memories to Meaning

The loss of a dear, close loved one can leave you feeling lost. After all, you have wrapped your life around them, and everywhere you turn reminds you of your loss. To navigate the pain, you try to hold on to your memories. What if you could use those memories to help you find meaning in your life moving forward?

In the initial throes of grief, we are in pain—and understandably so. As time goes on, we can surrender to the pain of loss. While having compassion for ourselves and what we have been through, we can think about what we can do to honor our loved one in the future. What did they stand for? What did they believe in? What did they value? Are these things you would like to focus on and incorporate into your own life moving forward? How might you make this happen?

Grief teaches us precious lessons. We start to understand the value of life and living life to the fullest. Suddenly, none of the petty stuff or drama matters. We get clarity around what does matter, and we focus on that. What matters is that our loved one lived, and they influenced us in a way that no one else has. They have left a unique imprint on our soul. We can use that to help honor them as we navigate life.

Blaine never waited around to do the things he wanted to do. He knew what he wanted. If I saw him eyeing a new truck or a new piece of machinery, I knew it was all but bought. Blaine loved people, and he loved visiting with people. He was genuinely interested in others and their lives, and he was not afraid to strike up a conversation with a stranger to find out more about them. He was a rancher.

Part of this lifestyle in our part of the world meant you helped your neighboring ranchers when it was time to brand the livestock. Every spring, he would attend several brandings. It meant good food and an opportunity to support and visit with others in the community. It was the highlight of every spring for people of all ages to attend the brandings. Blaine loved to travel, try new things, explore new ideas, and eat good food. He followed our kids around the country to watch them take part in hockey games or anything else they were doing. He attended their Christmas concerts, recitals, and track and field days. He loved being involved in our community and attending community events. He also loved hosting gatherings of family and friends at our home. Wing nights, brandings, and special holidays were the highlights of his life.

Knowing this about Blaine, I can look at my life and think about what he would love to see me carry out in mine. I can pick up on things he loved and integrate those things into my life in his honor. I can embrace life, meet new people, spend time with our kids and grandkids, and host events that welcome others. These things bring me joy. Even though I was reserved and quieter in my life with Blaine, I reach out more. Who would have thought I would become more social and travel to new places? As I stretch my wings, I learn new things. It brings me joy to help others, and I know Blaine sees me finding my way. I feel closer to him than ever, knowing he is by my side through it all. This gives me the confidence to forge ahead and continue to explore what possibilities exist in my future.

Trying New Things

After a significant loss, it is common for us to pull into ourselves and go into hiding. We play small. We get into a daily routine that feels safe, and we fall into complacency. Over time, we find ourselves bound by our own self-imposed limits. We allow others' expectations to trap us. For example, there might be an expectation for a widow to prioritize caregiving for children or other family members rather than pursue her own goals and expectations. Others might expect us to get along without support, yet the next well-meaning family member or friend might put pressure on us to continue to accept support that is just not helping us. We all have to recognize when something is not right for us anymore. At some point, we realize that doing the same thing we did yesterday serves us in one way and limits us in another. This is when we can consider stepping into the unknown and trying something new.

When I lost Blaine, I lived each day fearing I might not be able to do the things I needed to do to survive on my own. Some things, like fixing the lawn mower or lifting a heavy object into the back of the truck, were out of my scope. Fixing the water leaks and repairing the roof were beyond my ability, so I had to reach out to others. I had to rely on my family to help. I felt vulnerable and was worried about my future.

Something happens amid a drastic change. I have spent nearly two years contemplating the fact that I am a widow. Things have changed. I have changed. The situation leaves me no choice but to release any preconceived notions about how life should unfold. I must adapt and accept that I cannot control every situation. Still, it is difficult to accept change. I am sure caterpillars and tadpoles feel the same way when they metamorphose into butterflies and frogs. They have no choice but to surrender to the process. It must be frightening for them too, but I bet they could have never imagined what they would become!

Stepping out of your comfort zone can create anxiety. In the past, I was uncomfortable with making a mistake and looking foolish. I would rather have muddled through and figured things out myself than to have shown someone else what I did not know. In the past two years, calling a contractor or asking a neighbor for help made me nervous. Blaine used to take care of such things. *What if I fail? Will I make a wrong decision? Will I look stupid? What will others think of me? Will someone take advantage of me because of my lack of knowledge?* I think the fear of stepping into something we are not used to is always there. But I have learned that even though I have been a "play it safe" gal, I have a good head on my shoulders. That has served me well over the years, so why would it not serve me well in trying something new?

Is it time for you to try something new? It is never too late. Just like the butterfly, you never know how change will transform your life. Surrender to change. Surrender to something brand new.

New Relationships

At some point after losing a spouse, a person might consider finding another partner. There are a lot of factors that come into play in deciding whether this would be right for you. It is a personal decision. Marriage is a sacred act. It is a commitment. Both Blaine and I believed in the vows we took. Our marriage started out with all kinds of challenges. The night before our wedding, my brother, his best friend, and my cousin were in a dreadful accident. My brother's best friend was killed. My brother was okay physically. My cousin broke his arm. Both my brother and cousin were shaken up, and, of course, the entire community was in shock and grief. To add to the pain, Blaine got his fingers caught in the garage door when he was taking the car out. He had to go to urgent care for stitches. Also, we had just gotten a new little kitty, and a dog in the neighborhood ... well, ate the kitten.

Despite all of that, we went ahead with the wedding. As you can imagine, our wedding day was a blur of emotion, ranging from devastation, grief, and sorrow to excitement and joy. I look back at my wedding photos and wonder, *How did we ever get through that?* Our marriage started with grief and ended with grief, and there were moments of grief along the way. But the thirty-five years in between were filled with joy and happiness. We stayed together through it all. We loved each other dearly.

I have wondered whether I might consider having another partner someday. Being in the house alone has been a big adjustment. I wonder, at the age of fifty-six, what I might do with my life. Sometimes I feel too young to be a widow. I think many people would agree, but I guess there is never a good time to become a widow.

Not everyone has a conversation with their partner about what might happen in the event one person dies. I think we each secretly hope we will go first, or we will go together. The thought of living without our partner is too much to imagine. So, we might avoid that discussion due to discomfort. Regardless of the conversation you had or did not have, I believe that when our loved ones go home to the spirit world, they want us to continue to enjoy our earth time, whatever that looks like for us.

As spiritual beings, I believe we all came here to experience life on earth. Our spirit was excited to get here! We had plans to enjoy all that being in a human body has to offer. We were excited to experience life through our senses. As human beings, however, we cannot fathom why we would want to come to earth or experience grief and loss.

I look at this life like a brief holiday Blaine and I took together. In the scheme of universal time, this earth visit is short. Blaine and I agreed to meet and build this life together. We are soulmates. Blaine left his human body earlier than me and went home, but he is here in spirit. I feel him with me. When I am finished with my work here, I will join Blaine in the spirit world. Here on earth and in the spirit world, we have a special, magical relationship that is unique to us. Whatever choices Blaine or I make on our earth visits will not affect our relationship. That relationship is nested in unconditional love, and this love is forever.

I know there is more love than we can ever imagine. We never run out of love! We extend our love infinitely. This is why, when you have more than one child, you do not love the second one less than the first. I love Whitney as much as I love Curtise. I did not run out of love when she came along—I just increased my capacity to love more. For me, it is the same if we find another partner. We will never love our first partner any less. Nothing can take away the love we feel for them, the memories we had with them, and everything we shared. Blaine was the father of my children. He was special. He was my best friend and my greatest love. No one will ever take that away. However, if I were to meet someone new, I would love them too, and in a brand-new way I cannot possibly imagine. This is how love expands. This is how you expand.

As widows or widowers, we must consider our own healing before we decide to step into another relationship. Energetically, we want to be aware of the law of attraction. If we are jumping into a relationship because we cannot stand to be alone, or we are sad, or we are financially unstable, or because of any other problem, the relationship will hinge on that need. We must process all the emotions around our loss first and be comfortable with ourselves right where we are. Happiness does not come from outside of us. It is our inner being that brings us happiness.

When I went to Sedona the first time, I took part in an individual breathwork session. It took place in the evening, and it brought up such potent emotions that, by morning, I could have crawled right out of my skin. There was so much sorrow coming up. The thought of no longer having my best friend was eating me alive. Fortunately, I had the morning booked with a wise, compassionate shaman who said, "Angela, there is a goddess inside you that you need to get to know. She is your best friend. I will introduce you to her."

We went to a quiet place near a creek, and the shaman beat a drum while I went into a deep meditation. I realized I would have to get to know myself before I could ever think about connecting with another partner or finding another best friend. Letting go is a process, and when we are in a relationship, we identify ourselves as being intertwined as one. When we lose our loved one, we feel like a piece of us is missing. We think if we find another person to fill the gap, it will take the pain away. Perhaps it will, to a point. But we will lose out on the opportunity to get to be all we can be.

Before seeking a new partner, take the time to find out, "Who am I, truly?" Reflect on the needs, desires, and goals of the best friend within you. Being clear will allow you to attract the next relationship based on all that will enhance and enrich your goals and desires. It will not be about filling a void. It will be about expanding an already very rich life.

Many people who have lost a partner get into a new relationship and then find out they cannot let go of feelings of guilt for the betrayal of their loved one in spirit. It is hard (and perhaps impossible) to commit fully to someone new when you are busy trying to deal with powerful emotions that have not been released from the loss of a previous relationship.

We have to reach a level of acceptance regarding our loss. This does not mean forgetting or minimizing the significance of the relationship with your loved one but finding out what you believe about that relationship and how you want to move forward from it. Assessing your readiness to open up to new experiences, connections, and possibilities will help. You must be ready to meet new people, be strong enough to be vulnerable, and be patient enough to wait for someone who aligns with your own goals, desires, and values.

Everyone is going to have an opinion about whether you should "move on" and find someone new. Some people will tell you that you should start dating. Others will chastise you because you are dating. Some friends will question your actions, and some family might feel uncomfortable because of it. You have to be prepared for this emotionally. You have to trust you will make the best decision based on your choices and preferences. You must be strong enough to walk away if you do find a new partner and discover later they are not right for you. It is a lot to consider. In the end, it is your choice. You know what is best for you.

Exercise:

- Use this chart to write down a few things you would like to try.

What would I like to try?	What holds me back? (What must I consider first?)	What action to take? (A small step in that direction)

Follow up:

- Write down the names of support people who can direct you or assist you as you take action. How can you nurture yourself as you move through this process?

Chapter 15

Expanding into Your New Life

Human Resilience

Human beings adapt and recover from extremely challenging circumstances. Even after a devastating loss, we can find a sense of peace, meaning, and acceptance in our lives. We can find role models all around us who have transformed their lives in amazing ways through the grieving process. While I know I will still feel sad from time to time, the punched-in-the-gut feeling faded away when I embraced and accepted my new life.

As I have said, the grieving process can be a catalyst for personal growth and transformation. I have gained insight. I have developed a deeper understanding of myself and have found a renewed appreciation of life. I have grown and healed. I feel whole. It does not mean I have forgotten Blaine or the life we lived together. I will never forget the beautiful love we shared because I have integrated it into my life's story. I honor Blaine's memory deeply and carry everything I learned from my life with him into this new life. I have found a balance that incorporates the loss of my husband.

My loss has catapulted me onto a new trajectory. Through the transition, I have been forced to look at my values, my priorities, and ultimately, my life's purpose. My new sense of purpose has helped me find new meaning. My loss has also made me redefine my identity. I realize the Angela I am now was not possible before. I am grateful for the support my parents, my children, Blaine's family, my friends, and so many others have given me. I have had the privilege of working with my grief coach and many gifted energy healers. It has been my great honor to hold space for the Awaken Your Soul's Journey Community, as they have held space for me. We walk this path together and have only begun to recognize the profundity of our collaboration and connection.

Healing comes when we choose to move forward from our loss actively. Healing happens when we have realized who we truly are and move toward our purpose. At some point, the focus on our loss changes. The little black ball in the jar we once signified as pain and darkness becomes a heart full of love. We realize, in fact, that our spirit was never broken. It was always whole and complete and beautiful. Our human self may continue to have moments of sadness from time to time, and we acknowledge and meet that part of ourselves with love and kindness. Our spirit celebrates all we have gained through living a life with our loved one and all we continue to experience going forward.

The grieving process has guided me back to a life I enjoy. I continue to learn and grow with grief to guide me. Through grief, I have gained an understanding of something much bigger than I could have imagined. Through grief I have awakened to who I am. When you are ready, I wish for you to have what you need to design your next steps. I am excited for your future.

Planning the Future

To plan our future, we have to do things in manageable stages. Remember, we all progress through our grief in different ways, in our own time. Our grief is uniquely and perfectly designed for our own healing. You must trust the process, look after your needs, and seek support and guidance. As a cap-up of everything I have covered in this book, here is an outline of items that can help you think about how you might start taking small steps toward building your future.

1. Mourn your loss.
2. Practice self-care.
3. Seek support and connection.
4. Show patience and compassion for yourself.
5. Reflect on your values and priorities.
6. Explore new possibilities.
7. Allow your future to find you.

Below you will find additional reflection questions and exercises to help support you in each of the suggested action items listed above. These activities are designed to help you move into your future with more ease and grace.

When you start to take little steps in the direction of your future, something amazing happens. You start to see little synchronicities. A person will show up just when you need them, or some information will come to your attention in just the right way. You will start to recognize that these things are not coincidental. These little serendipities are your higher self letting you know you are being guided on the right path. You will start to trust that the answers will come when you need them and you will find yourself less anxious about your future. You will start to trust that there is something working for you and that if you just focus on following your joy, you cannot do anything wrong. As if by magic, you will see that life will get easier and more exciting. Will you still have challenges? Of course! Yet, you will see that those challenges are there to help you grow, and as difficult as they might be, you will learn to not resist them. You will allow them, knowing you have the full support of the team of guides, helpers, angels, and, of course, your loved ones in spirit, cheering you on all the way!

The following is overall guidance to continue your healing journey after reading this book and to begin to build a new life. Use these action items to help you reflect and determine next steps. Choose the activities that resonate with you to help you continue to move forward through the grieving process in order to build a new, fulfilled life you love again in your future.

Mourn your loss.

In my initial grief, I could not think about the future. I had to allow myself to mourn. The emotions come forward precisely when they are ready to be healed. It is important that when they do come, you express your grief.

- Find a place in nature such as a park or a beach. Bring a small, natural object that represents your grief or emotions, such as a stone, leaf, or feather. Set your intention of releasing the emotion of grief you have been carrying. Once you have taken time to reflect, take a few deep breaths and center yourself. Observe and connect with the nature around you, using as many senses as possible. Feel the ground beneath your feet. Visualize the emotion of grief as your object. Release that object into the water, bury it in the ground, or just set it at the base of a tree as a symbolic gesture of letting those feelings and emotions go. Visualize a healing energy coming from nature around you filling up the space where the grief once resided. Feel the peace and love that nature around you brings. Express gratitude out loud or in writing. Take deep breaths and embrace the sense of peace and renewal. Write about your experience in your journal or express it in another way. Repeat this exercise as often as it feels right to do so.

Practice self-care.

Self-care is crucial when you are grieving. It is not always easy to carry out self-care. In fact, sometimes it is the last thing we care to do. Yet we can choose to take self-care in very small steps. We do not do it because we feel like it. We do it because we know it is important. We make the choice out of love for ourselves. Doing one small thing can start the momentum for doing one more. I focused on my physical, emotional, and mental well-being by listening to my body and doing what brought me comfort, joy, and relaxation.

- What will bring you comfort? Will you go for walks, do an exercise routine, spend time in nature, travel to see family or friends? Will you write a blog? Create some form of art or do a craft? Make a list of the things that bring you comfort and help you look after yourself. What brings joy to each of us is unique. Explore some things to find what is right for you. You can always change it up as you find out what works best for you or as you get new ideas.

- When will you schedule time for these things? Will it be first thing in the morning? Will it be every day? What kind of time can you free up for yourself? Get a calendar and schedule what you plan to do for self-care and when. Make the tasks small. It is better to do something than nothing at all.

It is important to make this time sacred and set boundaries around the time. Make sure this is a priority and that it is fun for you. You should look forward to this time.

Seek support and connection.

We are not meant to do grief alone. I reached out for help and found support and connection through the speakers I interviewed for my summit and the audience, who have become part of my community. I also started participating in some groups in my own community. Consider reaching out to find your own connections.

- Make a plan to join at least one group. This might be online or in person. The first step is getting yourself out there. Remember, you are just exploring what works for you. You will need to make sure you find a balance between time for your own personal reflection and time for you to connect. Pay attention to your feelings and adjust accordingly. If you already belong to community groups, evaluate their importance to you. Choose what is best for you without worrying about what others think or if you will disappoint someone.
- The people who attend my online get-togethers provide empathy, encouragement, and understanding to one another and to me. We share our experiences and have built strong, immensely helpful connections. Feel free to join us.[20]

Show patience and compassion for yourself.

Planning for your future takes time. Each of us will awaken to our true self and start to seek purpose and meaning when we are ready. It is best to allow it to happen rather than try to force it. In the meantime, find things that bring you joy. Chase those. Accept moments of uncertainty.

- To build your confidence, write down some powerful statements to repeat daily whenever you are feeling uncertain. Words are powerful. Try putting sticky notes on your mirror that say things like "I am okay." "I got me." "I am on a creating journey." "I am worthy." "I am a good person." "I am enough." Say these out loud morning and night. Say them during the day when you think of it. It helps to stop the critical mind from taking over your thoughts.

Be kind and loving to yourself as you navigate the path to your future. There are no mistakes, only opportunities for growth.

Reflect on your values and your priorities.

I have found that helping others who are grieving has brought me purpose and fulfillment. Spending time with my family has become a priority. Learning about my spiritual self brings me joy. One way we can determine what is most important to us is to create a priority list.

- Make a list of all the tasks you need or want to achieve. These might be work-related tasks or personal ones. Add in family commitments and hobbies.
- Once you have the list, assign a level of importance to each item. Use a scale of 1 to 5, with 1 being the highest priority.
- Consider how your priorities are matching your values. If you need to determine your values, check the exercise at the end of Chapter 12. Do your priorities match your values? For instance, if one of your chosen values is commitment to family, how is that reflected in your list? You may need to adjust the priorities accordingly.

- Finally, create a plan to tackle your top priorities first. Remember to break them down into small steps.
- Your priorities can change over time. Revisit your list regularly to reassess. Make adjustments as needed.

Explore new possibilities.

When we sit in stillness and allow our feelings and emotions to come up, we can release them and open ourselves up for healing. With healing comes the opportunity for new experiences. If you had asked me two years ago if I would be doing what I do now, I would have said, "Not a chance." Life brings us challenges. With those challenges come great opportunities if we open ourselves up to them. Consider these questions:

- How can you turn your challenges into opportunities?
- How can you help yourself grow from your experience?
- What are some things you might consider trying?
- It does not matter if the answers do not come right away. Just allow your mind to think about these questions. It will help it open up to new ideas over time.

Allow your future to find you.

In our grief, it is hard to set goals right away. Goals can be restricting too. If we leave ourselves open to opportunity instead, there may be something we would not have thought of. For example, I did not set a goal to host an online summit on grief, yet it was an amazing and fulfilling experience. You do not have to know what your goal is going to be in life. You just have to be curious about what you want to try next. Once you determine that, you start the quest by discovering what is out there. Take a class or research something you are interested in. For me, saying yes to a class opened up new opportunities, which opened up more opportunities.

- Write down one or two opportunities you can say yes to.
- What excites you? See where it takes you.

Remember, as you start to move into your future, it is important to look back from time to time to see the progress you have made and celebrate the fact that you have made it to this point. You have made it to this place in your life after what is conceivably the worst thing you can imagine.

Please know, I do truly care. I know how hard it can be to get out of that downward spiral when a challenge arises that stops your momentum forward. Yet I also know there is no challenge too big to overcome when you have your spiritual guides and helpers walking with you. Ask them to lead you to the support you need going forward. Embrace all that comes, and allow it to transform you into who you are truly meant to be. You have everything you need inside of you!

Let me know how things work out. I am excited to hear from you! You can contact me by going to my website at www.healingenergy.world.

Lots of love,

—Angela

Bibliography

Beletsky, L. *The Bird Songs Anthology: 200 Birds from North America and Beyond.* San Francisco, CA: Chronicle Books, 2007.

Brooks, Garth, vocalist. "Unanswered Prayers." Recorded 1989, Track 7 on *No Fences*. Capitol Nashville, 1990.

Brown, R., and J. Kulik. "Flashbulb Memories." *Cognition* 5, no. 1 (1977): 73-99.

Cluff, Julie. *Miracles in the Darkness: Building a Life After Loss.* Springville, UT: CFI, an imprint of Cedar Fort, 2020.

Cuyler, Margery, and David Catrow. *That's Good! That's Bad!* New York, NY: Square Fish, 2012.

Doyle, Shawn. *The Sun Still Rises: Surviving and Thriving After Grief and Loss.* Shippensburg, PA: Sound Wisdom, 2014.

Harriott, Alain, and Jody Harriott, with Tyler Odysseus. *Energy Healing and the Art of Awakening Through Wonder*. United States: Alain & Jody Harriot with Tyler Odysseus, 2017.

Hay, Louise L. *You Can Heal Your Life*. Carlsbad: Hay House, 2017.

Jensen, Wendi J. *The Healing Questions Guide: Relevant Questions to Ask the Mind to Activate Healing in the Body*. Mesa, AZ: Inspired Body Network, LLC, 2015.

Kingston, Karen. *Clear Your Clutter with Feng Shui*. London, England: Piatkus, 2017.

Kübler-Ross, Elisabeth, and Ira Byock. *On Death and Dying: What the Dying Have to Teach Doctors, Nurses, Clergy and Their Own Families*. New York, NY: Scribner, 2019.

Lapolitano, Tia, Shonda Rimes, and Nzingha Stewart. *Gray's Anatomy*. Season 13, Episode 19, "What's Inside." April 16, 2017.

Mah, Kristie Anne. *The Day the Cancer Quit: A True Story of Surviving Stage IV Pancreatic Cancer*. Kendallville, IN: Kristie Anne Mah, 2020.

Moore, Tom T. *The Gentle Way: A Self-Help Guide for Those Who Believe in Angels*. Flagstaff, AZ: Light Technology Publishing, 2006.

O'Connor, Mary-Frances. *The Grieving Brain: New Discoveries About Love, Loss, and Learning*. New York: HarperOne, 2022.

Tolle, Eckhart. *The Power of Now: A Guide to Spiritual Enlightenment.* London: Yellow Kite, Hodder & Stoughton, 2020.

Your West Central Voice. "Commentary." Accessed August 30, 2024. https://www.yourwestcentral.com/commentary.

URLs (except where noted, all URLs accessed November 14, 2023).

Alexandria, Suzanne. "Suzanne Alexandria Enterprises – Home." Suzanne Alexandria Enterprises LLC. Accessed August 26, 2024. https://www.suzannealexandria.com/.

Anthony, Mark. "The Psychic Lawyer." Mark Anthony The Psychic Lawyer, 2020. https://www.afterlifefrequency.com/.

Awaken Your Soul's Journey. "Group Get Together." https://awaken-your-souls-journey-ukfjv1.mailerpage.io/group-support.

Baron-Reid, Colette. "Colette Baron-Reid." Oracle Cards, January 12, 2023. https://www.colettebaronreid.com.

Black, Joshua. *Awaken Your Soul's Journey* Podcast "Episode 6: Grief Dreams with Dr. Joshua Black." https://youtu.be/VAQJ-aJF0hc?si=jqPXqfDAvC5O0Ou5.

---. "Grief Dreams – Do You Dream of the Deceased?" Accessed August 29, 2024. https://www.griefdreams.ca/.

Blackwell, Adrien. Celebrity Healer Adrien Blackwell. Accessed August 29, 2024. https://adrienblackwell.com/.

Bowen, Sarah. "Why We Yawn and Why We Should Yawn More Often." Spirituality & Health, September 28, 2020. https://www.spiritualityhealth.com/articles/2020/09/28/12-reasons-to-yawn-every-day.

BrainyQuote.com. "Rumi Quotes." BrainyMedia Inc, 2023. Accessed December 15, 2023. https://www.brainyquote.com/quotes/rumi_597890.

Brown, Brené. "Dare to Lead List of Values." Brené Brown, November 14, 2023. https://brenebrown.com/resources/dare-to-lead-list-of-values/.

---. "Shame vs. Guilt." Brené Brown, January 15, 2013. https://brenebrown.com/articles/2013/01/15/shame-v-guilt/.

Clement, Angela. "Awaken Your Soul's Journey." *healingenergy.world*. Accessed December 15, 2023. http://www.healingenergy.world.

Clement, Angela. "Episode 6: Grief Dreams with Dr. Joshua Black." YouTube video, March 25, 2024. Accessed July 10, 2024. https://youtu.be/VAQJ-aJF0hc?si=OgQwaTXzLGZjdQ5y.

Cluff, Julie. "Grief Support." *juliecluff.com*, May 8, 2023. https://buildalifeafterloss.com/grief-support.

Coeur, Ana. "About." Ana Coeur, June 5, 2022. https://anacoeur.com/about/.

Dictionary.com. "Grief Definition & Usage Examples." Accessed November 10, 2023. https://www.dictionary.com/browse/grief.

Doyle, Shawn. "4 Ways to Be Happy Again after Losing a Loved One." *The Good Men Project*, July 18, 2021. https://goodmenproject.com/featured-content/4-ways-to-be-happy-again-after-losing-a-loved-one-dg/.

Eden, Donna. "Donna Eden's Daily Energy Routine [Official Version]." Energy Medicine. YouTube video, November 24, 2015. https://youtu.be/Di5Ua44iuXc?si=uPZs_cHBl5Q55ela.

Eden, Donna. "Figure 8's For Alleviating Pain." Energy Medicine. YouTube video, September 28, 2023. https://youtu.be/JqO-t1foCeQ?si=8KLSW3OQPm29ZdSZ.

Eden, Donna. "The Triple Warmer Smoothie for Fight, Flight, and Freeze Response." Energy Medicine. YouTube video, May 21, 2023. https://www.youtube.com/watch?v=4A56-hDhbDo.

Ferguson, Dr. Leshia. "Healing Roots – Naturopathic Clinic in Swift Current." Healing Roots – Naturopathic Clinic, April 4, 2022. https://healingrootsnd.com/.

Gardner, Cara. "Emotional and Mental Causes of Illness. The List by Louise Hay." Heartland Healing Arts, June 19, 2018. https://www.heartlandhealingarts.com/blog/2018/6/19/emotional-and-mental-causes-of-illness-the-list-by-louise-hay.

Hailley, Cathleena. "Home." Cathleena Hailley. Accessed August 29, 2024. https://www.cathleenahailley.com/.

Hay, Louise. "Hay Foundation: Louise Hay's Non-Profit Foundation." *Louise Hay*, September 9, 2015. https://www.louisehay.com/hay-foundation.

Hay, Louise L. *You Can Heal Your Life*. Bath: Camden, 2008.

Hawkes, Julie. "Emotion Cards." Life Balance, 2024. https://www.juliehawkes.com/emotioncards.

Henry, T. "Tyler Henry." *The Tyler Henry Medium*, 2024. https://www.thetylerhenrymedium.com.

Johnston, D. H. "The Wheel of Life." *Lessons4Living*, 1997. Accessed December 6, 2023. http://www.lessons4living.com/wheel_of_life1.htm.

Jensen, Wendi. Wendi Jensen Religious Recovery Coaching. Accessed August 26, 2024. http://www.wendijensen.com/.

Hawkes, Julie. "Home Page." Julie Hawkes Energy and Life Coaching. Accessed August 29, 2024. https://www.juliehawkes.com/.

Luftenegger, Paul. "International Conscious Singer, Songwriter, Composer, Heal Your Life® Teacher, and Reverend of Global Ministry." Dr. Paul Luftenegger, 2022. https://paulluftenegger.com/index.html.

Merriam-Webster. "Grief." Accessed November 10, 2023. https://www.merriam-webster.com/dictionary/grief#:~:text=%3A%20deep%20and%20poignant%20distress%20caused,life's%20joys%20and%20griefs.

Ortner, Jessica. "How to Tap with Jessica Ortner: Emotional Freedom Technique Informational Video." The Tapping Solution. YouTube video, April 11, 2013. https://www.youtube.com/watch?v=pAclBdj20ZU.

Oxford Learner's Dictionaries. "Oxford Advanced Learner's Dictionary." Accessed November 10, 2023. https://www.oxfordlearnersdictionaries.com/definition/english.

Prengel, Serge. "The Original Serenity Prayer by Reinhold Niebuhr." *Proactive 12 Steps*, May 27, 2022. https://proactive12steps.com/serenity-prayer/.

Pope, Dan Charles. "If You're Comfortable You're Not Growing." *Dan Charles Pope*, 2017. https://dancharlespope.wordpress.com/.

Rana, Vivek. "When the Ego Weeps for What It Has Lost, the Spirit Rejoices for What It Has Found." *Medium*, December 11, 2023. https://medium.com/@vivekpr/when-the-ego-weeps-for-what-it-has-lost-the-spirit-rejoices-for-what-it-has-found-6d0d5327b1e3.

Shapiro, Fred R. "The Chronical Review: Who Wrote the Serenity Prayer?" The Chronicle of Higher Education, April 28, 2014. https://www.chronicle.com/article/who-wrote-the-serenity-prayer.

Sise, Mary. "Align With Your Soul." Mary Sise LCSW, October 27, 2023. https://marysise.com.

Spirit Quest Sedona. "Spiritual, Healing, & Couples Retreats in Sedona, Arizona." SpiritQuest Sedona Retreats, July 19, 2024. https://retreatsinsedona.com/.

Tolle, Eckhart. "Spiritual Teachings and Tools for Personal Growth and Happiness." *Eckhart Tolle*, November 7, 2023. https://eckharttolle.com/.

Tonkin, Lois "Growing Around Grief—Another Way of Looking at Grief and Recovery." Bereavement Care, 15(1) p10, DOI: 10.1080/02682629608657376.

Tremblay, Joan. "Home." Joan Tremblay – Body Mind Spirit Energy Healing. Accessed August 29, 2024. https://joantremblay.ca/.

Waldman, Mark. "Mark Waldman – Video 1- Part3 - A 60 Second Exercise Will Reduce Stress and Anxiety." *Mentors and Motivators* by Lynn Kitchen. YouTube video, January 1, 2022. https://www.youtube.com/watch?v=sZjYvua6Nvc.

Williams, Lisa. Lisa Williams – Psychic Medium, Bestselling Author, Spiritual Teacher. Accessed August 29, 2024. https://lisawilliams.com/.

Vail, Melinda. "Home Page." Melinda Vail, Inc. Accessed August 29, 2024. https://melindavail.com/.

Endnotes

1 Rumi Quotes, "Rumi – Grief Can Be the Garden of Compassion. If You Keep…," Brainy Quote, accessed December 16, 2023, https://www.brainyquote.com/quotes/rumi_597890.

2 "Oxford Advanced Learner's Dictionary," Oxford Learner's Dictionaries, accessed November 10, 2023, https://www.oxfordlearners dictionaries.com/definition/english.

3 "Grief," Merriam-Webster, accessed November 10, 2023, https://www.merriam-webster.com/dictionary/grief#:~:text=%3A%20 deep%20and%20poignant%20distress%20caused,life's%20joys%20 and%20griefs.

4 "Grief Definition & Usage Examples," Dictionary.com, accessed November 10, 2023, https://www.dictionary.com/browse/grief.

5 Donna Eden's Daily Energy Routine, 2015, accessed August 26, 2024, https://youtu.be/Di5Ua44iuXc?si=uPZs_cHBl5Q55ela.

6 Triple Warmer Smoothie, accessed August 31, 2024, https://youtu.be/4A56-hDhbDo?si=8dR4oNh4Gpr8W0OF.

7 Tia Lapolitano, Shonda Rimes, and Nzingha Stewart, Gray's Anatomy, Season 13, Episode 19, "What's Inside," April 16, 2017.

8 Brené Brown, "Shame vs. Guilt," Brené Brown, October 10, 2023, https://brenebrown.com/articles/2013/01/15/shame-v-guilt/.

9 "Mark Waldman - Video1- Part3 - A 60-Second Exercise Will Reduce Stress and Anxiety," (Mentors and Motivators by Lynn Kitchen, 2022), https://www.youtube.com/watch?v=sZjYvua6Nvc.

10 https://youtu.be/JqO-t1foCeQ?si=8KLSW3OQPm29ZdSZ.

11 https://www.heartlandhealingarts.com/blog/2018/6/19/emotional-and-mental-causes-of-illness-the-list-by-louise-hay.

12 https://www.louisehay.com/hay-foundation/.

13 Vivek Rana, "When the Ego Weeps for What It Has Lost, the Spirit Rejoices for What It Has Found.*," Medium, December 11, 2023, https://medium.com/@vivekpr/when-the-ego-weeps-for-what-it-has-lost-the-spirit-rejoices-for-what-it-has-found-6d0d5327b1e3.

14 Sarah Bowen, "Why We Yawn and Why We Should Yawn More Often," Spirituality + Health, September 28, 2020, https://www.spiritualityhealth.com/articles/2020/09/28/12-reasons-to-yawn-every-day.

15 Roger Brown and James Kulik, "Flashbulb Memories," Cognition 5, no. 1 (1977): 73–99, https://doi.org/10.1016/0010-0277(77)90018-x.

16 Check out the Awaken Your Soul's Journey Podcast "Episode 6: Grief Dreams with Dr. Joshua Black," https://youtu.be/VAQJ-aJF0hc?si=jqPXqfDAvC5O0Ou5.

17 There is a link in the bibliography titled Grief Group Get-Togethers.

18 Brené Brown, "Dare to Lead List of Values," November 14, 2023, https://brenebrown.com/resources/dare-to-lead-list-of-values/.

19 Serge Prengel, "The Original Serenity Prayer by Reinhold Niebuhr," Proactive 12 Steps, May 27, 2022, https://proactive12steps.com/serenity-prayer/.

20 You can sign up here: https://awaken-your-souls-journey-ukfjv1.mailerpage.io/group-support.

About Angela

Angela Clement is a certified grief coach, speaker, writer, healer, and the creator of the online series "Awaken Your Soul's Journey." Formerly a school principal and distance-learning teacher, Angela's path shifted after an energy healer helped her young son recover from a rare disease. Inspired, she trained in multiple energy healing modalities to help others find their inner light and heal.

After losing her husband to colon cancer in 2021, Angela began her deep journey of grief and healing. Determined to support others, she launched her first online summit in 2022, and since then, she has interviewed over 100 experts on grief and spirituality. She became a certified grief coach and has built a compassionate online community offering one-on-one and group support to grieving people.

Angela enjoys camping trips that allow her to connect with the earth and find peace in the outdoors. Her love for travel helps her find inspiration and new perspectives. Angela finds comfort and healing in the soothing melodies of music and also has a deep appreciation for penguins and chocolate.

Angela shares her insights and experiences in her blog, newsletter, and monthly newspaper column. She also hosts a podcast where she interviews experts on grief and spirituality and creates online videos that address common challenges in the grieving process. With her unique blend of personal experience, spiritual insight, and practical tools, Angela helps others transform through a journey of healing, self-discovery, and renewed purpose.

Dear Grieving Soul,

You've already taken the first steps on your journey of healing through the grieving process, and there is so much more to explore. The path to healing is ongoing, and the possibilities for joy and purpose are endless. Are you ready to embrace this new chapter in your life? Dive deeper into resources at www.healingenergy.world to support and uplift you as you continue your healing journey.

Healing, like living, is all about the journey, not the final destination. This book marks just the beginning. Remember to lean on your support system as you move forward. Connect with me on my Facebook Page, "Awaken Your Soul's Journey," for ongoing support and community engagement. Follow my blog for more insights and reflections, sign up for my newsletter, and read my monthly newspaper column for guidance on navigating grief.

Ready to rediscover your inner strength and continue on the path to renewal? Join us online and keep moving forward on your healing journey. May your path be filled with hope, healing, and transformation.

Lots of love,

—Angela

www.ingramcontent.com/pod-product-compliance
Lightning Source LLC
Chambersburg PA
CBHW071602030726
47593CB00001BA/277